One Perfect Ingredient

MARCUS WAREING

WITH JENI WRIGHT

For my blue-eyed girl Jessie, who was born
on the last day of the shoot. Love, Dad x

LONDON NEW YORK MUNICH MELBOURNE DELHI

PHOTOGRAPHY BY DAVID LOFTUS

Project Coordinator and Food Stylist for Marcus Wareing: Chantelle Nicholson
Project Manager and Editor: Norma MacMillan
Project Art Editors and Designers: Smith & Gilmour
Illustrator: Emma Dibben

Managing Editor: Dawn Henderson
Managing Art Editor: Heather McCarry
Production Editor: Jenny Woodcock
Production Controller: Sarah Sherlock

First published in Great Britain in 2008 by Dorling Kindersley Limited
80 Strand, London WC2R ORL

Penguin Group (UK)

A CIP catalogue record for this book is available from the British Library

ISBN: 978 1 4053 2004 7

Colour reproduced by Altaimage, UK
Printed and bound in China by Hung Hing Printing Group Ltd.

Discover more at
www.dk.com

CONTENTS

FOREWORD

Nowadays, because we try to buy everything we need on one or two weekly shops, we tend to buy more food than we need. Overbuying creates waste, which really bothers me. It's something that didn't happen in our parents' day, and it never happens in a chef's kitchen. This got me thinking about basic ingredients and how we use them.

How often do we buy the same things week in, week out, without a clue what we're going to do with them? How often do we open the fridge, look at what we've bought, and wonder what on earth we're going to cook?

Opening the fridge door rarely provides inspiration, but I hope that opening this book will. It's a book about everyday ingredients – taking a raw ingredient and showing three simple, different, and exciting ways to cook it. It's also about taking the stress out of deciding what to cook, by starting with the ingredients and looking at them in a different way. Take the humble carrot. Hardly very exciting, but a perfect example – a useful, everyday vegetable that you can make into a cake, turn into a tangy salad, or serve up in a savoury galette.

I hope this book will inspire you, and give you fresh ideas about using familiar ingredients. It will save you having to think on your feet, because I've done it for you!

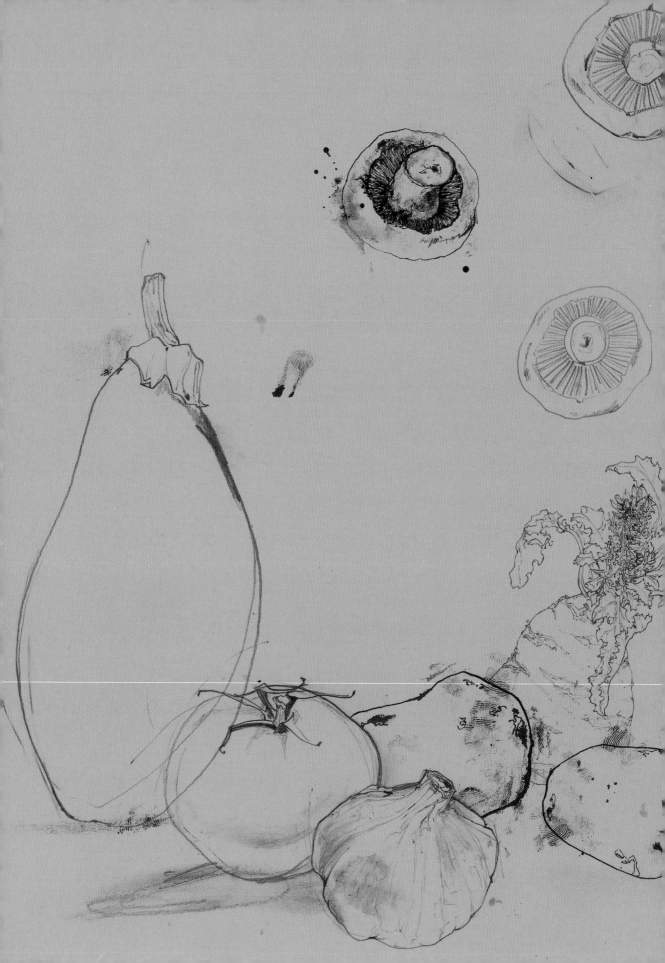

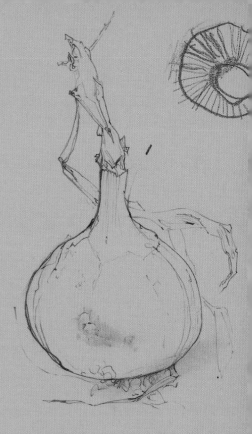

VEGETABLES

AUBERGINES

Choose fresh aubergines that are firm with smooth, shiny skins. They should "give" slightly when gently squeezed – this is how you know they're perfectly ripe. Overripe aubergines look wrinkled and dull, and the flesh inside will have lots of seeds. If you find aubergines slightly bitter for your taste, score the cut flesh, sprinkle with salt, and leave for 30 minutes. This will draw out any bitter juices, which you should rinse off before cooking.

2tsp cumin seeds
½tsp ground cinnamon
½tsp cayenne pepper
½tsp coarsely ground black pepper
Olive oil
2 aubergines, diced into bite-sized chunks
2tsp tomato purée
100ml hot chicken or vegetable stock
300g natural Greek yogurt
Sea salt and freshly milled black pepper

SERVES FOUR Chopped fresh coriander leaves, to finish

MOROCCAN AUBERGINES

Toast the spices in a dry large, deep frying pan over a low to medium heat for a few minutes until fragrant. Add a dash of olive oil, then stir in the aubergines and a pinch of salt. Fry over a medium to high heat for 5–8 minutes until the aubergines are tinged golden brown.

Stir in the tomato purée, then pour in the stock and stir again. Cover the pan and simmer for 10–15 minutes until the aubergines are soft, stirring occasionally. Taste for seasoning.

Add the yogurt and shake the pan gently to swirl the yogurt into the sauce, then sprinkle generously with fresh coriander. Serve hot or at room temperature.

1tsp garam masala

1tsp turmeric

1tsp ground cumin

1tsp black mustard seeds

Pinch of chilli powder, or more to taste

3 cardamom pods, crushed (both seeds and husks together),
or 1tsp ground cardamom

4tbsp vegetable oil

2 aubergines, diced into bite-sized chunks

1 onion, sliced

2 garlic cloves, crushed

½tsp fine salt

200ml hot chicken or vegetable stock

100g frozen peas

2tbsp chopped fresh coriander leaves

SERVES FOUR Sea salt and freshly milled black pepper

CURRIED
AUBERGINES
WITH PEAS

Toast the spices in a dry large, deep frying pan over a low to medium heat for a few minutes until fragrant. Stir in the oil, then add the aubergines, onion, garlic, and fine salt. Stir to combine with the spiced oil. Fry over a medium to high heat for 8–10 minutes, stirring frequently, until the aubergines almost begin to catch on the bottom of the pan.

Pour in the hot stock and stir to combine, then stir in the peas and seasoning. Cover the pan and simmer for 10–15 minutes until the aubergines are soft, stirring occasionally. Taste for seasoning and stir in the coriander just before serving.

As an alternative...use 500–600g okra, trimmed and sliced, instead of the aubergines.

1 aubergine
3 courgettes
1 large red pepper
1 large yellow pepper
2 red-skinned onions
2tbsp olive oil
2 garlic cloves, crushed
½tsp fine salt
4tbsp hot chicken or vegetable stock
2tbsp tomato purée
1tsp white wine vinegar
½tsp sugar (any type)

SERVES FOUR Sea salt and freshly milled black pepper

RATATOUILLE

Dice the aubergine and courgettes into 1cm squares so that each piece has some skin (you won't use the very centre of the aubergine). Dice the peppers and onions into pieces the same size.

Heat the oil a large, deep frying pan over a medium to high heat. Add the onions, garlic, and fine salt, and fry until the onions are almost soft. Add the peppers and courgettes, and cook for a couple of minutes longer. Now stir in the aubergine and stock. Simmer for a few more minutes before adding the tomato purée, vinegar, and sugar. Cook for another couple of minutes, stirring well, then add seasoning to taste. Serve hot or at room temperature.

BROCCOLI

The most common form of broccoli is calabrese, which takes its name from Calabria, the region in Italy where this vegetable originated. The heads should be tightly packed, with dark-green florets. Never overcook broccoli or it will lose its colour and texture. The best way to prevent this is to trim at least 50 per cent off the stalks so the florets are all the same size. This will ensure they cook evenly.

50g unsalted butter, diced
4 bay leaves
1 large head of broccoli, chopped into small pieces
1 litre hot chicken or vegetable stock
500ml milk
Sea salt and freshly milled black pepper

FOR THE CRUMBLE
125g sliced brown bread without crusts, toasted
125g blue Stilton cheese

SERVES FOUR

BROCCOLI SOUP WITH STILTON CRUMBLE

Melt the butter with the bay leaves in a large pan over a low heat. Allow to infuse for a couple of minutes, then add the broccoli and seasoning followed by the hot stock. Bring to the boil and boil for 1 minute. Discard the bay leaves and blitz in a blender. Pour into a clean pan and mix in the milk. Taste for seasoning. Set aside.

Get the grill hot.

To make the crumble, pulse the toasted bread in a food processor to make large, chunky crumbs. Crumble the cheese into a bowl and mix in the breadcrumbs.

Bring the soup to the boil, then ladle into flameproof bowls set on a baking tray. Dot the crumble on top. Grill until golden. Serve hot.

For a chunkier soup...only blitz half of the broccoli mixture. For a smoother soup...push through a fine sieve after adding the milk.

1 medium head of broccoli
100g blanched almonds, toasted
100ml extra virgin olive oil
Sea salt and freshly milled black pepper

Ciabatta toast (see below), to serve

BROCCOLI
AND TOASTED
ALMOND PESTO

Cut the head of broccoli in half lengthways, down through the stalk. Carefully shave off the very tops of the florets from one half using a sharp knife, to make a small amount of broccoli crumbs. Set the crumbs aside.

Break both halves of the broccoli into florets, then trim off the ends of the stalks. Plunge the florets into a pan of boiling salted water, bring back to the boil, and simmer for 4 minutes until just tender. Drain and plunge into a bowl of iced water. Leave to cool, then drain.

Put the almonds in a blender and chop until they look like coarse breadcrumbs. Add the oil and blanched broccoli florets, and pulse until just combined. Remove from the blender and fold in the broccoli crumbs with seasoning to taste.

Serve sprinkled with sea salt as a dip, with ciabatta toast on the side. Or use as a sauce for hot cooked pasta, adding a ladleful of the pasta cooking water to loosen it.

To make ciabatta toast...slice a ciabatta loaf. Drizzle olive oil on one side of each slice and place the slices oiled-side down on a hot griddle pan. Cook until they are marked underneath. Drizzle with more oil, turn over, and cook the other side. Sprinkle with salt and pepper before serving.

4 back bacon rashers
300g tenderstem broccoli, trimmed
100ml balsamic vinegar
4tbsp olive oil
50g pine nuts, toasted

Sea salt and freshly milled black pepper

BROCCOLI SALAD WITH BACON AND PINE NUTS

Heat the oven to 180°C fan (200°C/gas 6). Oil a baking tray.

Put the bacon rashers on the tray and place in the oven to cook for 8–10 minutes until just crisp.

Meanwhile, plunge the broccoli into a pan of boiling salted water, bring back to the boil, and simmer for 2–3 minutes until tender. Drain and refresh under the cold tap, then drain well again.

Simmer the vinegar in a small pan until the volume has reduced by half. Remove from the heat and swirl in the oil.

Pile the broccoli and bacon on plates, sprinkle with the toasted pine nuts and seasoning to taste, and drizzle over the balsamic dressing. Serve at room temperature.

CABBAGE

There are many varieties of cabbage, just three of which are cooked in totally different ways here. Apart from these, one of my all-time favourites is the pointed Hispi cabbage, which is at its best young in spring, when it needs only brief cooking. Sweet and juicy, it's everything you want a cabbage to be. Hispi is also good raw in mixed leaf salads, where it can provide an alternative texture to lettuce.

½ large Savoy cabbage, finely sliced
100g unsalted butter, diced
1 garlic clove, crushed
Light olive oil or vegetable oil
50g pine nuts, toasted
SERVES FOUR   Sea salt and freshly milled black pepper

SAVOY CABBAGE WITH NUT BUTTER

Plunge the sliced cabbage into a pan of boiling salted water. Leave for 30 seconds, then drain and refresh under the cold tap. Squeeze the cabbage to remove excess water and set aside.

Melt the butter in a small pan, then whisk over a high heat for 4–5 minutes until it turns pale brown and has a nutty aroma. At the same time, sauté the cabbage with the garlic in a little hot oil in a large, deep frying pan. When the cabbage is hot and nicely coloured, add the browned butter and toss to combine. Stir in the toasted pine nuts and seasoning to taste. Serve hot.

Vegetable oil
1 small red cabbage, weighing about 500g, finely sliced
1tsp fine salt
250ml red wine
250ml hot beef or vegetable stock
2 large Granny Smith or Bramley apples, peeled, cored,
    and finely sliced
2 garlic cloves
2 bay leaves
1 bunch of fresh thyme, tied with string
1tsp Chinese five-spice powder

Sea salt and freshly milled black pepper

SPICED RED CABBAGE WITH APPLE

Heat a little oil in a large, deep frying pan over a medium to high heat. Add the cabbage and fine salt, and sauté for a few minutes until the cabbage has wilted slightly. Pour in the wine and reduce by half. Now pour in the stock. Stir in the apples, whole unpeeled garlic cloves, herbs, and five-spice powder. Cover the top with non-stick baking parchment, turn the heat down to low, and leave to simmer gently for 25 minutes, stirring occasionally.

Remove the parchment and simmer the cabbage, uncovered, for a further 5 minutes until the liquid has reduced slightly. Discard the garlic cloves, bay leaves, and bunch of thyme, and taste the cabbage for seasoning before serving.

4 organic chicken breasts
4tbsp sweet chilli sauce
2tbsp toasted sesame oil
½ hard white cabbage
1 carrot
½ cucumber
200g beansprouts

FOR THE DRESSING
50g caster or granulated sugar
100ml white wine vinegar (or rice wine vinegar if you have it)
3 heaped tbsp sweet chilli sauce
1tbsp fish sauce
Juice of 1 lime

TO GARNISH
50g roasted peanuts, chopped
About 2tbsp roughly chopped fresh coriander leaves
About 2tbsp finely shredded fresh mint leaves

SERVES FOUR

ASIAN COLESLAW
WITH CHICKEN

Heat the oven to 180°C fan (200°C/gas 6).

Lay the chicken breasts in a single layer on a large sheet of foil. Spread them with the chilli sauce and sesame oil. Wrap the foil into a parcel and bake the chicken for 15 minutes. Cool, then shred or slice thinly on the diagonal, discarding any skin and bones. Set aside.

Slice the cabbage as finely as you can. Peel the carrot and cut into very fine julienne. Cut the cucumber in half lengthways and remove the seeds, then peel the flesh and cut into fine julienne. Mix all the cut vegetables in a bowl with the beansprouts.

To make the dressing, dissolve the sugar in the vinegar in a pan over a medium heat, then bring to the boil. Remove from the heat, add the remaining ingredients, and stir to combine.

Just before serving, add the chicken and dressing to the vegetables and toss together. Garnish with the peanuts and herbs.

For a quicker version...use ready-roasted chicken.

CARROTS

Don't just think of carrots as a vegetable to be cooked plain and served on the side – here they're used to make three completely different things with totally different flavours. And don't take them for granted because they're available all year round. Look out for new varieties and spend a little more money. The new season's carrots with their feathery tops are tender, with a sweet, nutty flavour.

700g carrots, peeled and coarsely grated
1tsp fine salt
150ml hot chicken or vegetable stock
1 onion, finely diced
Light olive oil or vegetable oil
3 medium organic eggs, beaten
60g Cheddar cheese, grated
2 heaped tbsp chopped fresh coriander leaves

SERVES EIGHT Freshly milled black pepper

CARROT AND CORIANDER GALETTE

Heat the oven to 180°C fan (200°C/gas 6). Line a 30 x 20 x 5cm baking tin with non-stick baking parchment.

Cook the carrots with the fine salt in a large, deep frying pan over a medium heat for about 20 minutes until the carrots are dry, stirring often. Pour in the stock and simmer for 10–15 minutes until it has all evaporated. Remove from the heat.

Cook the onion with a little oil in another pan until soft but not coloured. Mix into the carrots with all the remaining ingredients. Season well with pepper.

Spread in the baking tin in a smooth, even layer and bake for 15 minutes. Leave to cool for 5 minutes before slicing.

For a change from carrots...use celeriac, and change the coriander to chervil or flat-leaf parsley.

400g young carrots, peeled and cut into chunks on the diagonal
A few sprigs of fresh rosemary
4tbsp vegetable oil
200g baby carrots, peeled and left whole
6tbsp olive oil, plus extra for drizzling
2tbsp white wine vinegar
200g Chantenay carrots, peeled and left whole
50g unsalted butter, diced
100ml hot chicken or vegetable stock
1 shallot, sliced into thin rings
20g fresh tarragon, a few leaves kept whole and the rest chopped
20g fresh chervil, leaves chopped
125g feta cheese

SERVES FOUR Sea salt and freshly milled black pepper

THREE-CARROT
SALAD WITH FETA

Place the carrot chunks and rosemary sprigs in a frying pan with the vegetable oil. Season. Fry over a medium to high heat for 10 minutes until tinged brown and tender. Remove from the heat and set aside.

Bring a large pan of salted water to the boil. Add the baby carrots and boil for about 6 minutes until almost tender. Meanwhile, make a vinaigrette dressing by whisking 6tbsp olive oil with the wine vinegar and seasoning in a large bowl. Remove the baby carrots from the water with a slotted spoon and place straight into the vinaigrette. Set aside.

Using the same pan of water, boil the Chantenay carrots for about 6 minutes until almost tender. Drain in a colander and hold under the cold tap until cool.

Melt the butter in a frying pan over a medium heat, pour in the stock, and whisk until reduced to a sticky glaze. Add the Chantenay carrots and toss until they are glazed. Remove from the heat and stir in the shallot and chopped herbs.

Combine all three kinds of carrots together in a serving bowl. Season to taste and crumble the feta on top. Finish by drizzling with olive oil and sprinkling with sea salt and a few whole tarragon leaves.

If you can't get all three types of carrot…use just one or two varieties, or substitute parsnips, prepared and cooked as for the young carrots.

3 medium organic eggs
300g carrots, peeled and grated
4tbsp vegetable oil
125g Demerara sugar
50g walnuts, chopped

FOR THE FROSTING

175g plain white flour
75g plain wholemeal flour
1tbsp ground cinnamon
50ml milk
2tsp bicarbonate of soda

200g full-fat soft cheese
125g icing sugar, sifted
30g soft unsalted butter
Finely grated zest of 1 lemon
1tbsp lemon juice

CUTS INTO TEN SLICES

CARROT CAKE WITH CREAM CHEESE FROSTING

Heat the oven to 160°C fan (180°C/gas 4). Grease a deep 18cm round cake tin and set aside.

Beat the eggs in a large bowl, then add the carrots, oil, sugar, and walnuts. Mix well. In a separate bowl, combine the flours with the cinnamon. Gently stir the two mixtures together until half combined. Heat the milk in a pan until warm, then remove from the heat and stir in the bicarbonate of soda. Add this liquid to the cake mixture and stir together until just combined. Do not overmix.

Pour the mixture into the cake tin and bake for 30–35 minutes. Test if the cake is cooked by piercing the centre with a skewer: it should come out clean. If not, return to the oven and bake for a further 5 minutes, then test again. Leave to cool in the tin.

Place all the ingredients for the frosting in a food processor and process until smooth (or beat with an electric mixer or wooden spoon). Cover the cake all over with the frosting. Refrigerate until the frosting has set before slicing.

CAULIFLOWER

Only buy cauliflower that is firm and white. There should be no blemishes or softness. I think one of the nicest ways to eat cauliflower is raw with a dip. There's nothing to beat its unique crispness and flavour. For a change, look out for the new colourful varieties – the pointed, lime-green Romanesco is a good one, as are the mini cauliflowers with green or purple heads. Any of these can be used in the recipes here.

100g capers, drained
100g golden raisins
1 head of cauliflower, broken into medium-sized florets
SERVES FOUR · 1 punnet of red amaranth or purple radish, to garnish

CAULIFLOWER SALAD WITH CAPER AND RAISIN DRESSING

Place the capers and raisins in a pan with 100ml cold water and bring to a gentle simmer. When the raisins have plumped up slightly, tip the contents of the pan into a blender and blitz to make a smooth dressing.

Plunge the cauliflower into a large pan of boiling salted water. Bring back to the boil and simmer for 4–5 minutes until tender. Drain in a colander and hold under the cold tap until cool, then drain well again. Toss with the dressing. Serve straightaway, or refrigerate and serve chilled up to 24 hours later. Garnish just before serving.

If you can't get red amaranth or purple radish...use tiny purple basil leaves or basil seedlings instead.

1 head of cauliflower, weighing about 800g,
    broken into small, neat florets
2tbsp cumin seeds
Vegetable oil
½tsp fine salt
40g unsalted butter
40g plain white flour
450ml milk
75g mature Cheddar cheese, grated

Sea salt and freshly milled black pepper

CAULIFLOWER CHEESE WITH TOASTED CUMIN

Plunge the cauliflower into a large pan of boiling salted water. Bring back to the boil and simmer for 3 minutes. Drain, then plunge into a bowl of iced water. Drain again and spread out to dry on kitchen paper.

Toast the cumin seeds in a dry large, deep frying pan over a medium heat for a few minutes until fragrant. Tip out and crush with a pestle or the end of a rolling pin. Heat a little oil in the frying pan until just on the point of smoking. Add the cauliflower and fine salt, and toss over a high heat until browned. Toss in the cumin. Spoon into a flameproof dish.

Get the grill hot.

Melt the butter in a pan over a low heat, sprinkle in the flour, and mix well. Cook for a couple of minutes, then whisk in the milk a little at a time until smooth. Increase the heat and simmer for 5 minutes, whisking constantly, before stirring in about two-thirds of the cheese and some seasoning. Pour the sauce over the cauliflower, sprinkle with the remaining cheese, and grill until golden. Serve hot.

Instead of cauliflower...use 3 medium leeks. Trim off the roots and dark green tops, then slice into large chunks. Blanch for 1 minute only.

About 700ml milk
700ml chicken or vegetable stock
2 bay leaves
1 small bunch of fresh thyme, tied with string
1 head of cauliflower, roughly chopped

Fine salt

CAULIFLOWER SOUP

Bring the milk and stock to the boil with the herbs in a large pan.
Add the cauliflower, cover, and simmer gently for 15 minutes.
Remove the herbs.

Purée the soup in a blender until smooth, then pass through
a fine sieve into a clean pan. Add 1tsp fine salt and reheat the soup.
Stir in more milk if it is too thick. Taste the soup and add more
salt, if necessary. Serve hot.

Just as good...celeriac can replace the cauliflower.
Use 1 medium head, peeled and roughly chopped.

MUSHROOMS

All fresh mushrooms, whether cultivated or wild, are best on the day they're bought. If you have to keep them, take them out of any plastic packaging, which can make them sweat, and store them in a paper bag where it's cool and dry. They should keep well like this for a couple of days. Dried ceps (porcini) make good substitutes for fresh wild mushrooms when they're out of season. Their intense flavour is perfect for sauces, soups, and stews.

Olive oil
4 large field mushrooms
4 slices of country bread
4 large organic eggs
Vegetable oil

SERVES FOUR Sea salt and freshly milled black pepper

FRIED MUSHROOMS AND EGGS ON TOAST

Get the grill hot.

Heat a little olive oil in a large frying pan over a high heat. Add the mushrooms, gills facing down, and fry until darkly coloured. Turn the mushrooms over and fry the other side a bit, then sprinkle with sea salt and olive oil. Keep frying and turning until well coloured on all sides. The total cooking time should be about 10 minutes.

While the mushrooms are cooking, drizzle olive oil over the bread, season, and toast lightly under the grill. Turn the bread over and repeat on the other side.

In another pan, fry the eggs in a little hot vegetable oil until done as you like them.

Place a mushroom, gills facing up, on each piece of toast. Top with a fried egg and sprinkle with salt and pepper. Serve straightaway.

For a neat presentation...fry the eggs in round metal rings to contain the whites.

25g unsalted butter
50g walnut pieces or halves
400g button mushrooms, diced
Leaves picked from 1 small bunch of fresh thyme
100g full-fat soft cheese

Sea salt and freshly milled black pepper

MUSHROOM AND WALNUT DIP

Melt the butter in a frying pan over a medium heat and add the walnuts. Keep them moving in the pan for a few minutes to colour them slightly all over. Add half of the mushrooms with the thyme, season well, and cook for about 5 minutes until the mushrooms are soft.

Tip the contents of the pan into a food processor and pulse until the nuts have broken up. Add the remaining raw mushrooms and pulse a couple of times more. Transfer to a bowl and mix in the cheese. Taste and adjust the seasoning. Cover and keep in the fridge, then stir the dip well before serving.

Serve chilled, with crostini, breadsticks, or crudités, or use as a sandwich filling.

4 shallots, sliced
1 small bunch of fresh thyme, tied with string
100ml dry white wine
50ml brandy
25g dried ceps (porcini)
250ml hot chicken or vegetable stock
200ml double or whipping cream
Sea salt and freshly milled black pepper

SERVES FOUR

CREAMY CEP SAUCE

Place the shallots, thyme, wine, and brandy in a pan over a medium heat. Bring to the boil and reduce the liquid to a syrup. Add the ceps and stock, and simmer gently for 20 minutes. Remove from the heat and discard the thyme.

Blitz the sauce in the pan with a hand blender, or blitz in a food processor, then pass through a fine sieve into a clean pan. Add the cream and seasoning to taste, stir, and heat through. Serve with steak, chicken, or pasta.

For a foam finish...blitz the sauce with the hand blender in the pan while it's heating through.

ONIONS

An essential in every kitchen, onions are the starting point for so many savoury dishes, as well as being a main ingredient in their own right. White-skinned onions will make you cry when you cut them, but for cooking they're among the best. Tight and compact, they're the most flavoursome of all onions and the least watery, making them great for soups. Red onions look good and taste mild, and are best for using raw in salads.

100g unsalted butter, diced
4 large Spanish onions, about 400g total weight, finely sliced
½tsp fine salt
6 ripe large tomatoes, skinned, deseeded, and roughly chopped
1tbsp clear honey

**MAKES ABOUT
500ML**

2tsp white wine vinegar
Sea salt and freshly milled black pepper

ONION AND TOMATO MARMALADE

Melt the butter in a large pan until it begins to bubble. Add the onions and fine salt, and stir to mix with the butter, then let them sweat over a low heat until softened. Increase the heat and cook for about 45 minutes, stirring occasionally, until they caramelize to a deep golden colour. Add the tomatoes and cook slowly, stirring often, until the mixture reduces down and deepens in colour. This will take 20–30 minutes.

Transfer to a colander and leave to drain for about 30 minutes, stirring occasionally. Tip into a bowl. Mix in the honey, vinegar, and seasoning. Decant into sterilized Kilner jars and seal. Leave until cold before storing in the fridge for up to 1 month. Serve with cheese, quiche, or frittata.

To skin tomatoes...make a small cross in the base with the tip of a sharp knife, then plunge the tomatoes into a pan of boiling water and leave for 10 seconds. Remove and plunge immediately into a bowl of iced water. Lift out the tomatoes one by one and peel off the skins.

150g unsalted butter, diced
6 large white-skinned onions, finely sliced
1 bunch of fresh thyme, tied with string
1 head of garlic, cloves separated and peeled
600ml milk, plus extra for blanching
600ml chicken or vegetable stock
Sea salt

TO FINISH
A little double or whipping cream (optional)
Extra virgin olive oil

SERVES SIX

WHITE ONION
AND THYME
VELOUTÉ

Melt the butter in a large pan and add the onions and thyme. Sweat over a low to medium heat, stirring occasionally, for 15–20 minutes until all the liquid has gone. Take care not to let the onions colour.

Meanwhile, put the garlic cloves in another pan, cover with water, and add a pinch of salt. Bring to the boil, then drain and rinse under the cold tap. Repeat this blanching process, then repeat the blanching one more time using milk rather than water. Drain the garlic and refresh again in cold water.

Add the blanched garlic cloves to the pan of onions. Stir in 600ml each milk and stock, and bring to the boil. Remove from the heat and discard the thyme. Blitz the soup in a blender until smooth, then pass through a fine sieve into a clean pan.

To serve, reheat and add salt, if necessary. Finish by stirring in a little cream, if you like, and drizzling with olive oil.

50g unsalted butter
6 red-skinned onions, finely sliced
2tbsp fresh thyme leaves
1tsp fine salt
375g pack puff pastry
100g blue Stilton cheese

SERVES FOUR Freshly milled black pepper

RED ONION
AND BLUE
CHEESE TART

Melt the butter in a large, deep frying pan and sweat the onions with the thyme and salt over a low to medium heat for 20–30 minutes until they are soft and lightly coloured. Tip into a colander and leave to drain and cool. Season with pepper.

Line a baking tray with non-stick baking parchment. Roll out the pastry on a floured surface until 3mm thick. Cut out a 30 x 23cm rectangle. Place it on the parchment-lined tray and prick all over with a fork. Spread the cooled onions evenly over the pastry rectangle, leaving a 2cm border clear. Fold the border in to make a double-thickness "frame" all around, pressing to seal. Refrigerate for 30 minutes.

Heat the oven to 180°C fan (200°C/gas 6).

Bake the tart for 20–25 minutes until the pastry is golden. Crumble the cheese on top, then bake for a further 3 minutes until the cheese has just started to melt. Serve hot or at room temperature.

ONIONS

VEGETABLES

PEAS

The season for fresh peas is incredibly short, so watch out for them – the flavour of young peas fresh from their pods is incomparable. At other times of the year, frozen peas and petits pois are a godsend for bright colour and pop-in-the-mouth texture. Frozen within a few hours of picking, they can always be relied on for sweetness and tenderness.

400g shelled fresh or frozen peas
200g shelled fresh or frozen broad beans
100ml olive oil
4tsp white wine vinegar
2tbsp chopped fresh mint leaves
50g Manchego cheese, shaved
Sea salt and freshly milled black pepper

SERVES FOUR 2 large handfuls of pea shoots, to finish (optional)

PEA AND BROAD BEAN SALAD WITH MANCHEGO CHEESE

Plunge the peas and broad beans into a pan of boiling salted water. Bring back to the boil and simmer for 2 minutes until just tender, then drain and refresh under the cold tap. Drain well. If the broad bean skins are tough, peel them off with your fingers.

Whisk the oil and vinegar in a large bowl with salt and pepper to taste. Add the peas, beans, and mint, and toss together until evenly mixed. Taste for seasoning, then pile into a serving bowl. Top with the cheese and pea shoots (if using). Serve at room temperature.

500g frozen peas
300ml milk
2 medium organic eggs
About 2tbsp chopped fresh flat-leaf parsley
2 leeks (white part only), thinly sliced
4 large floury potatoes (eg King Edward or Maris Piper),
    peeled, thinly sliced, and rinsed
25g unsalted butter, melted

SERVES FOUR ½tsp fine salt

GRATIN DAUPHINOIS
WITH PEAS AND LEEKS

Heat the oven to 160°C fan (180°C/gas 4).

Tip the peas into a large pan of boiling salted water, bring back to the boil, and simmer for 1 minute. Drain the peas, then blitz to a purée in a blender with a little of the milk.

Whisk the eggs in a bowl. Add the pea purée, parsley, and remaining milk, and whisk to combine. Spread half of the pea mixture in a shallow baking dish (about 24 x 17cm and 4.5cm deep) and cover with half of the leeks. Mix the potatoes, butter, and salt together, then layer half on top of the leeks. Repeat the three layers.

Bake for 1–1¼ hours until the potatoes feel tender when pierced with a skewer. Leave to stand for about 5 minutes before serving.

Instead of peas…use sweetcorn kernels. If the sweetcorn is fresh or frozen, blanch it as for the peas; if you're using canned sweetcorn, drain and rinse well.

4 shallots, finely sliced
200g piece of rindless smoked streaky bacon,
   cut into small chunks
500ml hot milk
500ml hot chicken or vegetable stock
200g frozen peas
Sea salt and freshly milled black pepper

SERVES FOUR

PEA AND BACON VELOUTÉ

Sweat the shallots and chunks of bacon in a pan over a low heat for
10–15 minutes, stirring occasionally. Pour in the milk and half of the
stock and stir to mix, then remove from the heat. Cover with cling
film and leave to infuse for 1 hour.

Bring the remaining stock to the boil in a pan. Add the peas and
simmer for 2 minutes. Blitz to a purée in a blender. Mix with the
infused shallot and bacon mixture, then blitz in batches to a smooth
purée. Reheat in a clean pan and taste for seasoning before serving.

POTATOES

There are two types of potato – floury and waxy. Floury potatoes are the ones for roasting, mashing, baking, and chips, and the varieties to look out for are the white King Edward and Maris Piper, and the red-skinned Desirée. Waxy new potatoes hold their shape, so they're the ones for boiling and steaming, and for salads. Charlotte and Cara are two of the best. The new season Jersey Royals are in a class of their own – simply boil them and toss in butter.

1kg small new potatoes, halved or quartered if large
100ml olive oil, plus extra to serve
A few sprigs of fresh rosemary
1 head of garlic, cloves separated and peeled
100g pitted dried black olives with herbs, roughly chopped
Finely grated zest of 1 lemon

SERVES FOUR Sea salt and freshly milled black pepper

ROSEMARY ROAST POTATOES WITH OLIVES AND GARLIC

Heat the oven to 180°C fan (200°C/gas 6).

Put the potatoes in a roasting pan with 100ml olive oil, the rosemary, and seasoning. Mix well, then roast for 40 minutes until the potatoes are tender, adding the whole garlic cloves halfway through the cooking time.

Remove from the oven and stir through the olives and lemon zest. Serve hot, drizzled with extra olive oil and sprinkled with sea salt and fresh black pepper.

40g unsalted butter
3tbsp chicken or vegetable stock
800g large floury potatoes (eg King Edward or Maris Piper), peeled
2 shallots, finely sliced into rings
Sea salt and freshly milled black pepper

TO SERVE
2–3tbsp olive oil

1 small bunch of fresh thyme

BOULANGÈRE TERRINE

Heat the oven to 180°C fan (200°C/gas 6). Grease a 20–22 x 9–10cm baking tray or loaf tin that is 4–5cm deep. Line with non-stick baking parchment, making sure it fits tightly into the bottom edges.

Melt the butter in a small pan. Pour in the stock and simmer for a few minutes, whisking to make a creamy emulsion. Remove from the heat.

Using a mandolin, the slicing attachment of a food processor, or a very sharp knife, cut the potatoes into the thinnest possible slices. Place in a bowl and season. Brush the parchment with a spoonful of the emulsion, then place a double layer of overlapping potatoes evenly on this. Cover with a layer of shallots and brush with more emulsion. Repeat until the potatoes and shallots are used, finishing with the last of the emulsion.

Cover with foil and bake for 30 minutes. Uncover and bake for another 30 minutes until the potatoes are cooked and tender and starting to brown on top. Remove the tray from the oven, cover with another baking tray, and place heavy weights on top. (If you've used a loaf tin, place another tin on top and fill with weights.) Leave until cold.

To serve, lift the potato cake out of the tray on the paper, then cut into four slices. Heat the olive oil in a frying pan until hot, add the potato slices and sprigs of thyme, and fry until the potatoes are hot, spooning the hot oil over them, and turning the slices to brown both sides. Transfer to serving plates with a fish slice.

To make ahead of time...when cold, cover and keep in the fridge overnight.

To reheat the slices another way...place them on a lightly oiled baking tray and heat in the oven at 180°C fan (200°C/ gas 6) for 10–15 minutes.

4 large floury potatoes (eg King Edward or Maris Piper),
    about 800g total weight, peeled and quartered
1 medium organic egg, beaten
2tbsp chopped capers (optional)
1tbsp crème fraîche
2tbsp chopped fresh flat-leaf parsley leaves
2tbsp vegetable oil
25g unsalted butter, diced

Sea salt and freshly milled black pepper

POTATO CAKES

Place the potatoes in a pan of cold salted water and bring to the boil.
Lower the heat, cover, and simmer for 15–20 minutes until tender.
Drain and refresh under the cold tap.

When the potatoes are cold, crush them roughly with a fork in a
large bowl. Add the egg, capers (if using), crème fraîche, and parsley.
Season well. Mix everything together until evenly combined. Shape
into eight patties about 8cm diameter on a floured surface.

Heat 1tbsp of the oil in a non-stick frying pan. Add four potato cakes
and fry for 6–8 minutes on each side until golden. When turning the
cakes over, add half of the butter to the pan. Remove the cakes and
leave to drain on kitchen paper while frying the remaining potato
cakes in the same way. Serve hot.

To make ahead of time...shape into patties and keep
chilled until you're ready to cook.

Sweet potatoes...are equally good cooked this way.

TOMATOES

For cooking, use only really ripe, plump, and juicy tomatoes, and keep them out of the fridge so their aroma and flavour can develop to the full. I think ripeness is more important than variety, and it's best to buy vine-ripened tomatoes that are still on the vine if you can. These have an essence of the vine, which has an amazing aroma, and they taste like tomatoes really should.

1 small red pepper, finely sliced
1 shallot, finely sliced
Olive oil
1kg very ripe or overripe tomatoes, roughly chopped
1 small stalk lemongrass, halved and pounded
500ml tomato juice
5 drops of Tabasco sauce
1tbsp Worcestershire sauce
1tbsp balsamic vinegar, plus more to taste
A small handful of fresh basil leaves, torn
½ small watermelon, weighing about 750g, peeled and chopped
2 passionfruit, pulp only
Sea salt and freshly milled black pepper

SERVES EIGHT Extra virgin olive oil, to serve

TOMATO AND WATERMELON GAZPACHO

Sauté the red pepper and shallot in a little olive oil in a small pan for a few minutes until golden. Tip into a large bowl and add the remaining ingredients, except the watermelon and passionfruit. Mix together and season well. Cover and leave to infuse in the fridge overnight.

Purée the watermelon flesh in a blender. Add to the tomato mixture with the passionfruit pulp. Discard the lemongrass before blitzing the soup, in batches, in a blender until smooth. Pass through a fine sieve into a bowl. Taste for seasoning, and add more vinegar if you like.

Chill for a minimum of 4 hours. Serve chilled, sprinkled with a few drops of extra virgin olive oil.

If you have leftover soup...it freezes well for up to 3 months.

2kg very ripe or overripe tomatoes, cored and roughly chopped
500ml tomato juice
4 shallots, finely chopped
1 garlic clove, crushed
15g bunch of fresh thyme, tied with string
2 bay leaves
50g sugar (any type)

MAKES ABOUT 4tbsp white wine vinegar
1 LITRE Sea salt and freshly milled black pepper

TOMATO FONDUE

Cook the tomatoes, tomato juice, shallots, garlic, and herbs in a large, heavy pan over a medium heat, stirring occasionally, until thickened and reduced by about half. This will take 30–60 minutes, depending on the ripeness of the tomatoes.

Remove the herbs. Purée the contents of the pan in a blender, then push through a fine sieve into a bowl.

Heat a heavy frying pan over a high heat until hot. Add the sugar and melt over a low to medium heat, without stirring, then turn up the heat a bit and cook the sugar syrup until it turns to a golden caramel. Add the vinegar and swirl to combine. Stir into the purée. Season to taste and leave until cold. Use the tomato fondue as a sauce for pasta or as the base for a pizza topping, or in vegetarian lasagne.

If not using straightaway...store in sterilized Kilner jars in the fridge for up to 2 weeks.

2tbsp olive oil
1 punnet ripe cherry tomatoes
1 onion, finely diced
2 garlic cloves, crushed
1tsp sugar (any type)
100ml dry white wine
200g mascarpone

Sea salt and freshly milled black pepper

CHERRY TOMATO AND MASCARPONE SAUCE

Heat the oil in a large, deep frying pan over a high heat. Add the whole tomatoes and fry until they begin to burst, then add the onion and garlic and turn the heat down slightly. Soften the onion for about 5 minutes. Add the sugar and wine, and reduce to a syrup.

Add the mascarpone and shake the pan gently until the mascarpone melts into the tomatoes. Blitz in the pan with a hand blender. Season to taste before serving with pasta, poultry, or meat.

If you prefer...leave the sauce chunky, and don't bother with the blending at the end.

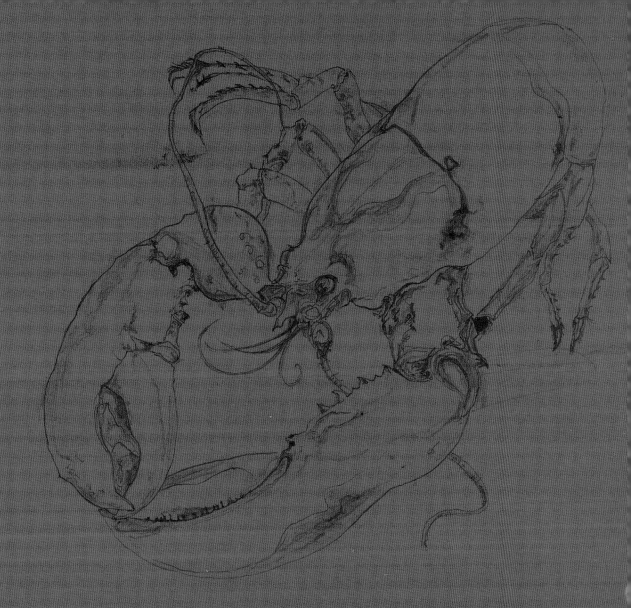

FISH & SHELLFISH

WHITE FISH FILLETS

Always buy freshly cut fillets from your fishmonger or supermarket fish counter – don't buy fish in packets because you can't see exactly what you're getting, and you don't know how long ago it was prepared. Haddock, cod, and sea bass are used in the recipes here in three different ways. Fillets from other white fish, such as halibut and monkfish, both of which are readily available, can be substituted, as can John Dory, sea bream, snapper, or red mullet.

½ large Savoy cabbage, finely sliced
200ml whipping or double cream
2tbsp vegetable oil
4 haddock fillets, without skin
25g unsalted butter, diced
2tbsp grainy mustard

SERVES FOUR Sea salt and freshly milled black pepper

PAN-FRIED HADDOCK WITH CREAMY MUSTARD CABBAGE

Plunge the cabbage into a large pan of boiling salted water. Bring back to the boil and simmer for 1 minute. Drain in a colander and hold under the cold tap until cool, then drain again and squeeze out the excess water. Set the cabbage aside.

Simmer the cream in a large pan over a medium heat until reduced by one-third. Meanwhile, heat the oil in a large non-stick frying pan over a high heat until hot. Season the fish well and sear quickly on both sides. Add the butter and cook the fish for 2–3 minutes more on each side, then remove the fillets from the pan with a fish slice and keep them hot.

Add the mustard and cabbage to the pan of cream and toss until the cabbage is hot. Taste for seasoning, then serve with the fish.

275g piece of cod fillet, without skin
1tsp fine salt
250g floury potatoes (eg King Edward or Maris Piper),
    peeled and finely sliced
125ml extra virgin olive oil
1 head of garlic, cut crossways in half
2 bay leaves
1 bunch of fresh thyme, tied with string
85ml milk
150ml whipping or double cream
2 leaves gelatine
Sea salt and freshly milled black pepper

TO SERVE
2 heaped tbsp chopped fresh flat-leaf parsley leaves
100ml extra virgin olive oil, plus a little more for drizzling
6 thin slices of ciabatta bread
Fresh thyme leaves

SERVES SIX

BRANDADE

Sprinkle the fleshy side of the cod with the fine salt and set aside.
Place the potato slices in a pan with the olive oil, garlic, and herbs.
Add 85ml cold water. Cover with non-stick baking parchment and
cook over a medium heat for about 20 minutes until all of the liquid
has been absorbed and the potatoes are tender.

Add the fish, milk, and cream to the potatoes and stir to mix.
Cover with parchment again and continue cooking for 5–8 minutes
until the cod is almost done. Meanwhile, soak the gelatine in a bowl
of cold water for 5 minutes.

Remove the pan of fish and potatoes from the heat and discard
the garlic and herbs. Lift the gelatine out of the water and squeeze
to remove excess moisture, then add to the fish and potatoes and stir
until melted. Purée the contents of the pan in a blender until smooth.
Push through a fine sieve into a bowl, and taste for seasoning. Cover
and refrigerate for at least an hour.

To serve, blitz the parsley in a blender with 100ml olive oil and a
pinch of sea salt. Toast the ciabatta slices and drizzle with olive oil,
then sprinkle with sea salt and a few thyme leaves. Transfer the
brandade to a bowl, top with parsley oil, and serve with the toast.

57

2tbsp olive oil
6 sea bass fillets, without skin

FOR THE CRUST
100g pine nuts, toasted
65g soft unsalted butter
1tbsp chopped fresh chervil leaves
1 garlic clove, crushed
Sea salt and freshly milled black pepper

FOR THE VINAIGRETTE
50ml red wine
50ml red wine vinegar
100ml extra virgin olive oil

SERVES SIX

SEA BASS WITH A PINE NUT CRUST AND RED WINE VINAIGRETTE

First make the crust. Blitz half of the pine nuts in a food processor until they are finely ground. Add the butter, chervil, and garlic, and blitz again to make a paste. Add the remaining pine nuts and pulse just until they break up. Season to taste. Place the mixture between two sheets of non-stick baking parchment on a tray and spread out evenly using a rolling pin until 3–5mm thick. Place in the freezer until frozen. Cut into six pieces the same size as the fish fillets, then return to the freezer until required.

To make the vinaigrette, reduce the wine to a thick syrup in a small pan over a medium heat. Add the vinegar and simmer for 5 minutes. Add the oil and remove from the heat.

When you are ready to cook the fish, get the grill hot.

Heat the olive oil in a large frying pan. Season the fish, then fry for 30 seconds on each side. Transfer, skinned-side up, to an oiled baking tray. Place a piece of the crust on top of each fillet. Grill for a few minutes until the crust is golden brown and bubbling. Serve with the vinaigrette.

SOLE

This flat white fish comes in two types – lemon and Dover. Lemon sole is the smallest and least expensive. It's the one you're most likely to find all year round as whole fish or fillets, and in some supermarkets you can buy skinned whole fish, which makes preparation easier. Dover sole is a great fish to cook and eat whole off the bone. Another common flat white fish is plaice, which you can use in any recipe calling for sole.

4 lemon sole fillets, without skin, each
    cut lengthways in half
3tbsp olive oil
1 onion, finely sliced
2 garlic cloves, crushed
150g piece of chorizo sausage
1tsp smoked paprika
500ml hot chicken or vegetable stock
400g can butter beans, drained and rinsed
Sea salt and freshly milled black pepper

SERVES FOUR

SOLE WITH BUTTER BEAN AND CHORIZO HOTPOT

Roll up the sole fillets into paupiette shapes, with the skinned side facing in, and secure with wooden cocktail sticks. Heat 2tbsp of the olive oil in a flameproof casserole or deep sauté pan and soften the onion and garlic over a low to medium heat. Meanwhile, remove the skin from the chorizo; thinly slice one-third of the sausage and chop the rest.

Sprinkle the paprika and seasoning into the pan, then add the chopped chorizo and cook, stirring, for 5 minutes. Pour in the stock and bring to the boil. Simmer gently for 10 minutes.

Stir in the butter beans. Place the sole paupiettes on top and spoon over a little of the simmering broth. Cover the pan tightly and simmer for 8–10 minutes to cook the fish. Meanwhile, pan-fry the chorizo slices in the remaining olive oil until crisp, then drain on kitchen paper.

Lift out the sole and remove the cocktail sticks. Stir the broth and taste for seasoning. Serve the bean hotpot topped with the sole paupiettes and garnished with the chorizo slices.

4 small lemon sole fillets,
  without skin
Vegetable oil, for deep-frying

FOR THE BEER BATTER
100g plain white flour
100g cornflour
½tsp fine salt
200–300ml ice-cold lager

FOR THE MAYONNAISE
1 medium organic egg yolk
½tsp Dijon mustard
Finely grated zest and juice of ½ lemon
100ml vegetable oil
100ml extra virgin olive oil
About 25g capers, finely chopped
Sea salt and freshly milled black pepper

SERVES FOUR

SOLE IN
BEER BATTER

First make the batter. Sift the flour, cornflour, and fine salt into a bowl, then slowly whisk in enough lager to make a smooth batter. Cover and refrigerate until required.

To make the mayonnaise, combine the egg yolk, mustard, and lemon zest in a bowl. Mix the two oils together in a jug. Using an electric mixer or hand blender, work the oil into the yolk mix, trickling it in very slowly at first. Once the mayonnaise starts to emulsify, add the remaining oil in a thin, steady stream. Add the capers, lemon juice, and seasoning to taste and mix well. Cover and keep in the fridge until serving time.

Cut each sole fillet lengthways in half, then cut each piece crossways in half to make 16 pieces in total.

Heat the oil in a deep-fat fryer to 180°C. Whisk the batter, then dip four or five pieces of fish into it until well coated. Lower the fish into the hot oil and deep-fry for 2–3 minutes until crisp and golden. Remove with a slotted spoon and drain on kitchen paper while you cook the remaining fish. Season and serve with the mayonnaise.

If you haven't got a deep-fat fryer...use a deep, heavy saucepan and test the temperature of the oil by dropping in a teaspoonful of batter. If it bubbles and turns golden in 20–30 seconds, the oil is at the correct temperature.

1tsp ground cinnamon
1tsp fennel seeds
2 star anise, roughly chopped
1tsp coarsely ground black pepper
1tsp whole cloves
1tsp fine salt
½tsp caster sugar
2 whole lemon sole, each weighing about 200g,
    skinned on both sides, head and tail removed
2tbsp olive oil

SERVES TWO
25g unsalted butter, diced

FIVE-SPICE SOLE

Toast the spices in a dry frying pan over a low to medium heat for a few minutes until fragrant. Tip into a spice grinder or blender and blitz until finely ground. Shake through a fine sieve to remove any large particles.

Mix the spices with the fine salt and sugar, and sprinkle over both sides of each sole. Heat the oil in a large frying pan (or in two medium pans) over a medium to high heat, add the sole, and cook for 2½ minutes on each side. Add the butter, let it foam, and serve.

Scallops and sole fillets...can be cooked the same way as the whole fish. They will only need 1½ minutes on each side.

PRAWNS

Raw prawns in their shells are far superior to ready-cooked prawns, because you can control the way you cook them. Tiger prawns should have a bite – the exact opposite of the cooked pink prawns you buy, which are almost always soft and mushy. When a dish requires the heads and shells to be removed before the prawns are cooked, don't throw these away. Use them in fish stocks and soups – they're invaluable for their flavour.

12–16 uncooked whole
    prawns in their shells
15g fresh coriander
1tbsp vegetable oil
1tbsp toasted sesame oil
2 x 400ml cans coconut milk
100g medium egg noodles
100–150g mangetout, cut
    crossways in half
100g beansprouts
50g roasted peanuts,
    roughly chopped

FOR THE SPICE PASTE
2 red chillies, roughly chopped
    with the seeds
1 stalk lemongrass, finely sliced
100g roasted peanuts
80g fresh root ginger, peeled
    and roughly chopped
2 garlic cloves, roughly chopped
1 onion, roughly chopped
4tbsp fish sauce
50g caster or granulated sugar
1tsp fine salt

SERVES FOUR

PRAWN LAKSA

Twist the heads off the prawns, peel them, and remove the black intestinal veins. Set the prawns aside in the fridge. Remove the leaves from the coriander and chop finely.

Roughly chop the coriander stalks and put in a blender or food processor with all of the paste ingredients. Pulse to a chunky paste.

Heat the vegetable and sesame oils in a deep pan over a medium heat. Add the spice paste and stir-fry for 5 minutes. Pour in 300ml cold water and bring to the boil, then simmer for 15 minutes. Add the coconut milk and bring back to the boil. Pass through a fine sieve into a clean pan. Bring the laksa to a gentle simmer and taste – you may want to add more fish sauce, sugar, or salt. Keep over a low heat.

Plunge the noodles into a large pan of boiling salted water. Bring back to the boil and simmer for 3–4 minutes until almost *al dente*. Drain and add to the laksa with the prawns. Simmer for 3–4 minutes until the prawns turn pink, stirring in the mangetout towards the end of the cooking time so they retain their crunch.

Ladle into bowls and garnish with the beansprouts, peanuts, and chopped coriander leaves. Serve hot.

12 uncooked whole tiger or jumbo prawns in their shells
6 slices of pancetta or Parma ham
Vegetable oil

FOR THE AÏOLI
1 head of garlic, cut crossways in half
Olive oil, for drizzling
1 medium organic egg yolk
½tsp Dijon mustard
2tsp white wine vinegar
¼tsp caster sugar
¼tsp fine salt
150ml vegetable oil
50ml extra virgin olive oil
Paprika, to finish

SERVES FOUR   Sea salt and freshly milled black pepper

PANCETTA PRAWNS
WITH ROAST
GARLIC AÏOLI

Heat the oven to 180°C fan (200°C/gas 6).

First make the aïoli. Put the garlic, cut-side up, on a large sheet of foil, season, and drizzle with a little olive oil. Fold over the foil to make a parcel. Roast for 20 minutes until very soft. Cool slightly, then squeeze the garlic flesh into a bowl.

Add the egg yolk, mustard, vinegar, sugar, and fine salt, and blitz with a hand blender or mixer to combine. Mix the oils together in a jug, then work into the yolk mix, trickling the oil in very slowly at first. Once the mayonnaise starts to emulsify, add the remaining oil in a thin, steady stream. Taste for seasoning, then cover and refrigerate until needed.

Twist the heads off the prawns and remove the shells, leaving the last tail section on. Remove the black intestinal veins. Cut the pancetta slices in half lengthways and wrap a piece around each prawn, leaving the tail shell exposed. Keep in the fridge until you are ready to cook.

Heat a little vegetable oil in a frying pan over a medium to high heat. Season the prawns, then fry, turning them occasionally, for 3–4 minutes until the pancetta is crisp and the prawns are pink. Drain on kitchen paper and serve hot with the aïoli, dusted with paprika.

For a change from prawns...use monkfish cut into pieces that are roughly the same size as prawns.

24–30 uncooked whole prawns in their shells
Vegetable oil
1 onion, roughly diced
1 carrot, roughly diced
1 celery stick, roughly diced
1 leek (green part only), roughly diced
1 stalk lemongrass, finely sliced
4tsp tomato purée
250ml dry white wine
2 litres hot chicken or vegetable stock
1 small bunch of fresh tarragon, tied with string
50ml brandy
200ml whipping or double cream

TO FINISH
Fresh coriander leaves
Splash of Pernod
Extra virgin olive oil

SERVES SIX
Sea salt and freshly milled black pepper

PRAWN BISQUE

Twist the heads off the prawns and remove the shells, leaving the last tail section on; reserve the heads and shells. Remove the black intestinal veins. Keep the prawns in the fridge until you are ready to cook them.

Heat a little oil in a frying pan over a high heat until almost smoking. Add half of the prawn heads and shells and cook for a few minutes until golden brown, stirring occasionally. Transfer to a colander. Repeat with the remaining heads and shells.

Place a large pan over a medium to high heat. Add a little oil, then add the onion, carrot, celery, leek, and lemongrass. Sauté until the vegetables are golden brown. Add the tomato purée and seasoning, and stir. Pour in the wine and simmer until reduced by about half. Pour in the stock. Drop in the browned prawn heads and shells and the tarragon. Bring to the boil, skimming off any oil or scum. Turn the heat down to low and simmer gently, uncovered, for 25 minutes.

Meanwhile, heat a little oil in a frying pan and cook the prawns over a high heat, turning them occasionally, for 3–4 minutes until they are pink and tinged golden brown. Drain on kitchen paper and keep hot.

Strain the simmering liquid into a clean pan. Add the brandy, cream, Pernod, and seasoning, and bring to the boil.

To finish, divide the prawns among bowls and scatter coriander leaves around them. Quickly blitz the bisque with a hand blender until frothy. Ladle around the prawns. Sprinkle with olive oil and pepper, and serve.

For a cold soup...chill the bisque in the fridge after cooling, then serve garnished with cucumber shavings.

SALMON

Raw, cured, or cooked – salmon can be enjoyed in three different ways. Wild salmon has more flavour than farmed, but its leanness can make it dry. Fattier farmed salmon is a safer option for the home cook, as the fat makes the fish juicier. When buying farmed salmon, check it isn't too fatty by looking closely at the fish. If you can see translucent, creamy fat around the edges, don't buy it.

1 side of salmon, weighing about 750g, with skin

FOR THE MARINADE
400ml fresh orange juice (from a carton is fine)
1 whole lemon, roughly chopped
1 whole orange, roughly chopped
125g caster or granulated sugar
90g rock salt
1tsp coriander seeds
1tsp white peppercorns
Leaves picked from 50g bunch of fresh dill

TO FINISH
1½–2tbsp Dijon mustard
Leaves picked from 125g bunch of fresh dill, chopped
Rock salt

SERVES EIGHT

GRAVADLAX

Blitz the marinade ingredients in a blender or food processor until quite smooth. Place the salmon, skin-side down, in a plastic tray and check for pin bones, then pour over the marinade. Shake the tray gently to ensure the entire piece of fish is covered. Wrap the whole tray tightly in several layers of cling film and refrigerate for 48 hours.

To finish, unwrap the salmon and rinse off the marinade under the cold tap. Pat the fish dry with kitchen paper. Spread the salmon with a very thin layer of Dijon mustard and pack the chopped dill on top, pressing it down firmly with your hands. Sprinkle very lightly with rock salt. Slice thinly to serve.

Vegetable oil
1 piece of salmon fillet, weighing 300–400g, with skin
1 small watermelon, weighing about 1.5kg
150g watercress, tough stalks removed
220g can water chestnuts, drained and roughly chopped
Sea salt and freshly milled black pepper

FOR THE VINAIGRETTE
5tbsp extra virgin olive oil
Finely grated zest of 1 lemon
3tbsp lemon juice

TO FINISH
50g fresh almonds, skinned and shredded (optional)
Finely grated zest of 1 lemon
Extra virgin olive oil

SERVES FOUR

THREE-WATER
SALMON

Heat the oven to 180°C fan (200°C/gas 6).

Heat a little vegetable oil in a large, ovenproof frying pan over a medium to high heat. Season the salmon well on both sides, then place, skin-side up, in the pan. Leave for 2 minutes, then turn the salmon over. Transfer to the oven to cook for 6–8 minutes, according to how you like your salmon. Remove from the oven and flake the salmon into large pieces, discarding the skin. Set aside.

Make a vinaigrette dressing by mixing the olive oil with the lemon zest and juice and seasoning to taste.

Peel the watermelon and slice thinly into discs, removing as many seeds as you can. Arrange the slices in a serving dish, overlapping them slightly. Pile the watercress in the centre and surround with the water chestnuts. Top with the salmon and drizzle over the vinaigrette. Finish by sprinkling over the almonds (if using) followed by the lemon zest and a little olive oil and sea salt.

For a more casual presentation...cut the watermelon into chunks and toss gently with all the other ingredients in a large salad bowl.

4 pieces of salmon fillet, each weighing 175–200g
and of equal thickness, with skin
50g rock salt
About 500ml light olive oil

Sea salt, to serve

CONFIT SALMON

Lay the salmon fillets, skin-side down, in a plastic tray. Sprinkle
the rock salt over the fish, then refrigerate for 2 hours.

Rinse the salt off the salmon under the cold tap. Pat the fish
dry with kitchen paper.

Place the pieces of salmon, skin-side down, in a deep, heavy
pan. Pour in enough olive oil just to cover the fish. Place the pan
over a low heat and warm the oil to 50°C. Leave for 15 minutes,
checking the temperature regularly with your thermometer.
You will need to move the pan off the heat frequently, to keep
the temperature of the oil constant at 50°C.

When the 15 minutes is up, gently turn the salmon over and
peel back the skin. If it comes off easily, the salmon is done; if
not, it may need another 5 minutes or more in the warm oil.

To serve, lift each piece of salmon out of the pan and gently
shake off excess oil. Discard the skin, then sprinkle the fish
lightly with sea salt.

TUNA

It's important to know that tuna is very fresh – it should look a rich, meaty red. With most other fish you can check for freshness by looking at the eyes and gills, but you never see a whole tuna, so you need to trust your supplier. Despite its meatiness, tuna is delicate and should never be overcooked. Control the cooking by searing, the best way to ensure the fish remains rare in the centre.

1 piece of tuna loin, weighing 400–500g
2tbsp vegetable oil
4tsp toasted sesame oil
Sea salt and freshly milled black pepper

FOR THE HUMMUS
100g dried white beans (cannellini or haricot), soaked
    in cold water overnight, then drained and rinsed
1 carrot, cut in half
1 onion, cut in half
1 small bunch of fresh thyme, tied with string
4tbsp tahini
1tsp fine salt

SERVES FOUR

SEARED TUNA WITH WHITE BEAN HUMMUS

First make the hummus. Put the beans in a pan with the carrot, onion, and bunch of thyme. Cover with cold water and bring to the boil. Cover the pan and simmer for 1–1½ hours until the beans are tender. Drain, reserving the cooking liquid. Discard the vegetables and thyme.

Blitz the beans in a blender with the tahini and fine salt, adding enough of the cooking liquid to make a smooth purée.

Heat the oven to 180°C fan (200°C/gas 6).

Pat the tuna thoroughly dry, and season with salt and pepper. Heat the vegetable oil in a frying pan over a medium to high heat. When the oil is hot, place the tuna in the pan and sear quickly on all sides – this should take 7–8 minutes in total. Transfer the tuna to a foil-lined baking tray and place in the oven to cook for 5 minutes. Meanwhile, warm the hummus over a low heat, stirring, and taste for seasoning.

Remove the tuna from the oven and cut into eight slices. Place a spoonful of hummus on each plate, top with two tuna slices, and drizzle with 1tsp sesame oil. Sprinkle with sea salt and serve.

1 long, slim piece of tuna loin,
  weighing 200–300g
Vegetable oil
1tbsp Dijon mustard
2tbsp chopped fresh coriander leaves
2tbsp chopped fresh chervil leaves
2tbsp chopped fresh flat-leaf parsley leaves
Sea salt and freshly milled black pepper

SERVES FOUR

FOR THE PINEAPPLE
1 small pineapple
100g caster or granulated sugar
2 star anise
10 black peppercorns

TO SERVE
Extra virgin olive oil
Ground cardamom
Fresh coriander leaves

HERB-CRUSTED
TUNA CARPACCIO

First prepare the pineapple. Top and tail the fruit, cut off the skin, and remove the "eyes". Slice the pineapple lengthways into very thin rectangles. Place in a large, shallow rigid container. Put the sugar and spices in a pan with 150ml cold water and heat gently until the sugar has dissolved. Bring to the boil and simmer for 5 minutes. Cool for 5 minutes, then pour over the pineapple. Cover and refrigerate until required.

Pat the tuna thoroughly dry, and season with salt and pepper. Place a non-stick frying pan over a high heat and pour in 2mm vegetable oil. Heat until almost smoking, then place the tuna gently in the pan. Sear for 1 minute until caramelized underneath. Pick the tuna up with tongs and turn it on its side. Sear as before, then repeat on the other two sides. The total searing time should be no more than 5 minutes. Transfer the tuna to a board and spread all over with a thin, even coating of mustard.

Place a roll of cling film at the back of the work surface and pull the film towards you to cover the work surface. Mix the herbs together and sprinkle over the film immediately in front of you. Place the tuna on the herbs and roll it until it is evenly coated in herbs. Now roll up the tuna very tightly in the film, wrapping it round several times, to make a taut sausage shape. Cut off the film, then twist at both ends of the sausage like a Christmas cracker. Refrigerate for at least 1 hour, or overnight.

To serve, slice the tuna into twelve 5mm-thick discs. Arrange a slice of pineapple on each plate and top with three slices of tuna. Sprinkle with olive oil and sea salt, and garnish with cardamom and fresh coriander.

Leftover slices of pineapple...make a refreshing snack, or they can be served with vanilla ice cream for a dessert.

1 piece of tuna loin, weighing 200–300g
3tbsp extra virgin olive oil
1tbsp white wine vinegar
50g pitted black olives, finely chopped
1tbsp finely chopped fresh dill leaves
4tbsp crème fraîche
Sea salt and freshly milled black pepper

FOR THE PICKLED CUCUMBER
100g caster or granulated sugar
100ml white wine vinegar
½ cucumber, very thinly sliced into discs with a vegetable peeler
3tbsp chopped fresh dill

FOR THE BALSAMIC TOAST
¼ baguette, sliced very thinly on the diagonal
3tbsp balsamic vinegar

SERVES FOUR

TUNA TARTAR
WITH PICKLED
CUCUMBER

First make the pickled cucumber. Dissolve the sugar in the vinegar in a pan over a low heat, then bring to the boil. Cool. Pour over the cucumber and dill in a shallow dish. Cover and refrigerate for at least 4 hours.

Arrange the cucumber slices, overlapping, on individual plates and sprinkle lightly with some of the pickling liquid. Set aside.

Toast the baguette slices. Drizzle with the vinegar and keep warm.

Cut the tuna into 5mm dice, using a very sharp knife and washing it often to prevent sticking. Put the tuna in a bowl and mix in the olive oil, vinegar, olives, dill, and seasoning.

To shape each serving, stand a metal ring, about 5cm in diameter and 7.5cm tall, on a board. Spoon in one-quarter of the tuna mixture, pressing it down well. Top with 1tbsp crème fraîche and a grinding of black pepper. Gently slide a palette knife under the ring and transfer to one of the plates of cucumber. Carefully lift off the ring. Repeat to shape the remaining three servings. Sprinkle the balsamic toast with sea salt and serve with the tuna tartar.

If you haven't got a metal ring...use an empty plastic drum that's a similar size – from an ingredient like bicarbonate of soda, baking powder, or dried herbs. Cut off the base and trim the drum to size, if necessary.

BROWN SHRIMPS

Potted shrimps – brown shrimps in butter – have always been relatively easy to get, but now more and more fishmongers and supermarkets are selling peeled, cooked brown shrimps loose. The best British shrimps come from Morecambe Bay in Lancashire, where they are trawled from the sea on tractors and boiled on the beach. Their flavour and texture are amazing.

2tbsp olive oil
100g unsalted butter, diced
200g peeled, cooked brown shrimps
A squeeze of lemon juice
1 garlic clove, cut into slivers
2 heaped tbsp finely shredded fresh
    flat-leaf parsley leaves
Sea salt and freshly milled black pepper

FOR THE TOAST
2–3 slices of ciabatta bread
Olive oil
1 garlic clove, peeled
Fresh thyme leaves

SERVES TWO

SAUTÉED SHRIMPS ON TOAST

Start making the toast. Drizzle the bread with olive oil, then toast in a hot griddle pan until lightly charred underneath. Drizzle with more oil and turn the bread over to toast the other side.

While the toast is cooking, heat the olive oil and half of the butter in a frying pan over a high heat. Add the shrimps with some seasoning and toss to mix with the oil and butter. Squeeze lemon juice over, then add the garlic, parsley, and remaining butter. Let the butter melt and foam, spooning the juices over the shrimps. Remove from the heat.

Rub the toast with the garlic clove, and sprinkle with thyme leaves, salt, and pepper. Spoon the shrimps over the toast and serve.

1 ripe mango
1 cooked lobster tail, shelled and cut
    crossways in half
2 cooked lobster claws
200g peeled, cooked brown shrimps
A small handful of baby rocket leaves
1 whole nutmeg, for grating

FOR THE VINAIGRETTE
4tbsp extra virgin olive oil
1tbsp rice wine vinegar
Sea salt and freshly milled black pepper

SERVES TWO

SHRIMP SALAD WITH MANGO AND LOBSTER

Peel the mango and remove all the flesh from the stone. Cut the flesh into thin slices. Dice a couple of the slices and set aside.

Divide the sliced mango between two plates, overlapping the slices slightly. Place a piece of lobster tail in the centre of each serving and surround with the meat from the lobster claws, the shrimps, diced mango, and rocket.

Whisk the vinaigrette ingredients together and drizzle over the salad. Finish by grating nutmeg liberally all over.

For a less formal presentation...gently toss all the ingredients together in a large salad bowl, and grate the nutmeg liberally on top.

250g ready-rolled puff pastry
200g peeled, cooked brown shrimps
100g white crab meat
3tbsp mayonnaise
2–3tbsp chopped fresh chives
Juice of ½ small lemon
1 small ripe avocado
Juice of ½ lime
5tbsp crème fraîche

Sea salt and freshly milled black pepper

SHRIMP AND CRAB TIAN WITH AVOCADO

Heat the oven to 180°C fan (200°C/gas 6). Line a large baking tray with non-stick baking parchment.

Re-roll the pastry on a floured surface until 3mm thick, then cut into a 28 x 15cm rectangle. Place the rectangle on the parchment and cover with another sheet of parchment. Set another heavy baking tray on top to keep the pastry flat. Bake for 7–10 minutes.

Remove from the oven and lift off the top tray and paper. Cut out four 5cm discs and four 4cm discs from the pastry, leaving them on the paper lining. Discard the pastry trimmings. Replace the paper and top tray on the discs and bake for a further 7–10 minutes until golden and crisp. Remove the top tray and paper and leave to cool.

Mix the shrimps with the crab, mayonnaise, chives, lemon juice, and seasoning to taste.

Halve the avocado and remove the stone, then scoop the flesh into a bowl. Add the lime juice and 1tbsp of the crème fraîche, and blitz with a hand blender until smooth. Season to taste.

To shape each tian, place a 5cm pastry disc on a serving plate. Stand a metal ring, about 5cm in diameter and 7.5cm tall, on top of the pastry. Fill with one-quarter of the shrimp mixture, pressing it down well. Carefully lift off the ring and top the tian with 1tbsp crème fraîche, smoothing it over. Now place a 4cm pastry disc on top. Finish with a quenelle of avocado purée and a grinding of black pepper. Repeat to shape the remaining three tians.

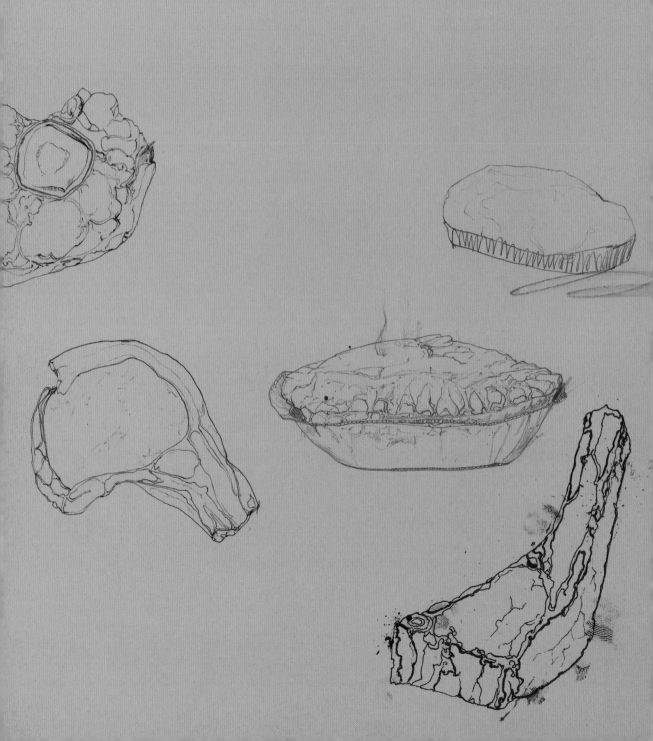

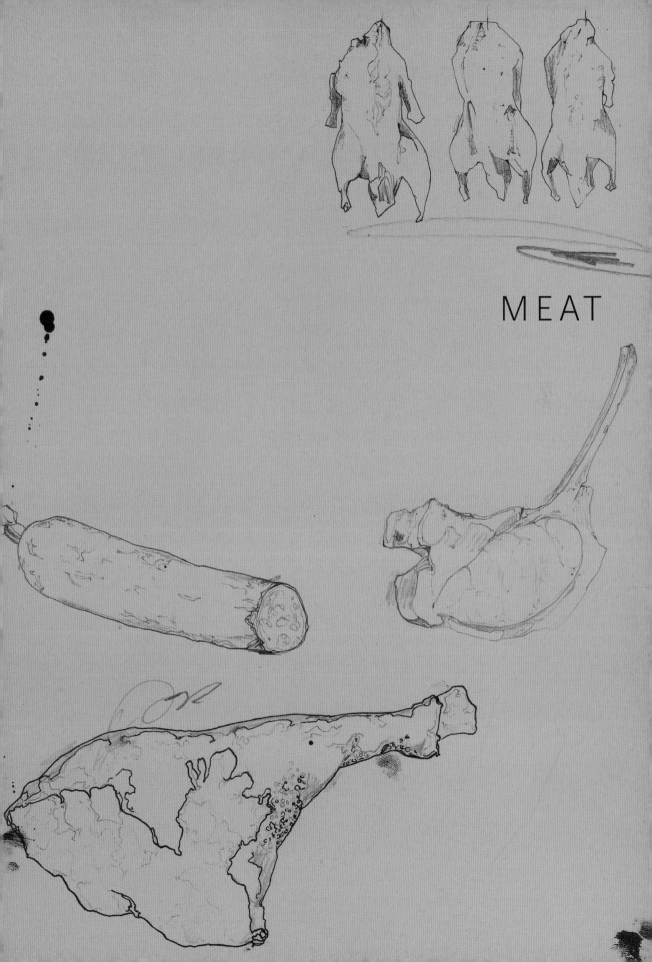

MEAT

BEEF

When choosing beef, look for a light marbling of fat throughout the meat, and creamy fat surrounding joints and steaks. Beef that has been hung is best for flavour and tenderness – well-hung beef is the colour of claret wine, not bright red. A good butcher will tell you about the meat's provenance, and will advise on cuts, cooking methods, and timings – vital information for successful results.

SERVES FOUR

1 piece of boneless beef rib eye,
     weighing about 1kg
100ml olive oil
1 small bunch of fresh thyme
1 small bunch of fresh rosemary
1 head of garlic, cut crossways in half
Cherry tomatoes on the vine and
     salad onions, to serve

FOR THE SHALLOTS
3tbsp vegetable oil
750g shallots, peeled, with roots kept on
2 bay leaves
A few sprigs of fresh rosemary
200ml port
100ml hot beef stock
Sea salt and freshly milled black pepper

BARBECUED RIB EYE

Place the beef in a plastic bag with the olive oil, herbs, and garlic. Seal and leave to marinate in the fridge overnight. About 1 hour before cooking, remove from the fridge.

To prepare the shallots, heat the oil in a large frying pan over a medium heat and add the shallots, bay leaves, and rosemary. Season. Cook for about 10 minutes until coloured all over. Add the port and reduce to a syrup. Stir in the stock and boil until reduced by half. Tip on to a doubled large sheet of foil and twist into a parcel like a money bag.

Light the barbecue. When the flames have died down, the coals are white, and the temperature is medium, you're ready to cook.

Remove the beef from the marinade and season well. Place on the grid of the barbecue with the marinade herbs. Cook for 45–60 minutes for medium-rare (the cooking time depends on your barbecue and the thickness of the meat). Turn the meat over every 15 minutes, including on to its fat side, and try to keep the heat at an even temperature during cooking. You may need to move the grid farther away from the heat, or push the meat to the edges of the grid, or even lift the meat off for a few minutes if the heat gets too intense.

Put the shallot parcel on the barbecue grid after the first 30 minutes, and add some tomatoes and salad onions towards the end of the cooking. Rest the meat in a warm place for 5–10 minutes before slicing to serve.

6tbsp vegetable oil
2 onions, finely chopped
2 garlic cloves, crushed
200g button mushrooms, quartered
500–600g braising steak
Seasoned plain flour, for coating
200ml red wine
600ml hot beef stock
4tbsp brown sauce
A dash of Worcestershire sauce
1 small bunch of fresh thyme
2 bay leaves
500g small new potatoes, peeled and
cut into chunks

SERVES FOUR Sea salt and freshly milled black pepper

FOR THE PASTRY
200g plain white flour
Pinch of fine salt
100g cold unsalted butter, diced

FOR THE VINEGARED ONIONS
About 400ml malt vinegar
1 large Spanish onion, finely
sliced into rings

MUM'S HOTPOT

Heat the oven to 140°C fan (160°C/gas 3).

Heat 2tbsp of the oil in a 2-litre flameproof casserole. Add the onions and garlic with a little fine salt, and fry until light golden. Remove with a slotted spoon and reserve. Add another 2tbsp oil and fry the mushrooms in the same way. Add to the onions.

Cut the beef into large cubes and coat in seasoned flour. Heat the remaining oil in the pan and fry the beef, in two batches, until well browned all over. Remove and reserve. Pour in the wine and scrape the pan to loosen the browned bits. Simmer until a syrupy consistency, then add the stock, sauces, and herbs. Stir well and bring to a simmer. Return the onions, mushrooms, and beef to the pan. Cover and place in the oven to braise for 2 hours, adding the potatoes halfway.

Now make the pastry. Sift the flour and salt into a bowl. Rub in the butter. Slowly mix in 3–4tbsp cold water to make a stiff dough. Wrap and refrigerate for at least an hour. Remove 15 minutes before using.

For the vinegared onions, gently warm the vinegar in a pan, tip into a large bowl, and stir in the onions to immerse. Cover and set aside.

Remove the casserole from the oven and cool for about 30 minutes. Increase the oven temperature to 180°C fan (200°C/gas 6).

Roll out the pastry and cut out a lid about 2.5cm larger than the diameter of the casserole. Discard the herbs from the casserole, and taste the gravy for seasoning. Brush water around the rim of the pan. Place the pastry lid on top, sealing well to the edge, and brush all over with water. Pierce a hole in the centre. Return to the oven to cook for 25–30 minutes until the pastry is a deep golden brown. Leave to rest in a warm place for 10 minutes before serving with the onions.

2 large oxtails, each cut into 4 joints
Plain flour, for coating
About 150ml vegetable oil
1tsp fine salt
About 1 litre hot beef stock
3 turnips
3 parsnips
3 carrots
1 head of garlic, cut crossways in half
1 small bunch of fresh thyme,
   tied with string
A small handful of bay leaves
Sea salt and freshly milled black pepper

FOR THE MARINADE
1 small bunch of fresh thyme
2 bay leaves
2 cinnamon sticks
2 onions, roughly chopped
1 carrot, peeled and roughly chopped
75cl bottle full-bodied red wine
   (Merlot or Cabernet Sauvignon)

SERVES FOUR

BRAISED OXTAIL
WITH RED WINE

Make the marinade: tie the thyme, bay leaves, and cinnamon together to make a bouquet garni and place in a bowl with the onions and carrot. Add the oxtail, then pour in the wine. Cover and refrigerate overnight.

Lift out the oxtail and dry on kitchen paper, then coat in flour. Strain the wine into a pan (reserve the vegetables and bouquet garni) and bring to a gentle simmer, skimming off the scum that rises to the surface.

Meanwhile, heat 3tbsp oil a large flameproof casserole over a medium to high heat and sear the oxtail, in two batches, until browned on all sides. Add more oil to the pan as needed. Set the oxtail aside.

Brown the marinated vegetables in the same pan. Pour in the wine and simmer until reduced by half. Add the reserved bouquet garni and the fine salt, then return the oxtail to the pan. Pour in enough stock to cover. Press a disc of non-stick baking parchment over the surface of the liquid, and keep at a gentle simmer for 2½–3 hours until the meat is very tender, regularly skimming off the fat that rises to the surface.

Meanwhile, peel the root vegetables and cut them in half or into large chunks, depending on their size. Heat 4tbsp oil in a large, heavy frying pan over a medium to high heat. Add the vegetables with the garlic, thyme, and bay leaves. Season well, then cook until browned.

When the oxtail is tender, add the root vegetables and stir well. Cover with parchment again and cook for 40 minutes until the vegetables are tender. Skim off the fat and taste the gravy for seasoning before serving.

If you prefer...the casserole can be cooked in the oven at 140°C fan (160°C/gas 3).

500g spinach, tough stalks removed
Fine salt
6 sheets of dried lasagne
50g Cheddar cheese, grated

FOR THE MEAT SAUCE
1 onion, finely chopped
2 garlic cloves, crushed
1 sprig of fresh rosemary
Light olive oil or vegetable oil
500g lean minced beef
400g can tomatoes, sieved
100g salted black beans
1tsp sugar (any type)
1tsp sweet chilli sauce

FOR THE CHEESE SAUCE
40g unsalted butter
40g plain white flour
500ml milk
1 bay leaf
1 whole nutmeg, for grating
50g Cheddar cheese, grated
Sea salt and freshly milled black pepper

SERVES SIX

LASAGNE WITH SPINACH AND BLACK BEANS

Plunge the spinach into a large pan of boiling salted water. Bring back to the boil and simmer for 1 minute. Drain in a colander and shake under the cold tap until cool. Squeeze to remove excess water.

Next, make the meat sauce. Soften the onion with the garlic and rosemary in a little oil in a large, deep frying pan over a medium heat. Add the mince and brown lightly, breaking up any lumps. Stir in the tomatoes, black beans, sugar, and chilli sauce. Simmer over a low heat for 15–20 minutes until reduced to a rich sauce. Discard the rosemary.

While the sauce is simmering, heat the oven to 180°C fan (200°C/gas 6). Cook the lasagne sheets, one at a time, in a large pan of boiling salted water for 2 minutes. Drain. Run under the cold tap until cool.

For the cheese sauce, melt the butter in a pan over a low heat, sprinkle in the flour, and mix well. Cook for a couple of minutes, then whisk in the milk a little at a time until smooth. Add the bay leaf and grate in as much nutmeg as you like. Increase the heat and simmer for 5 minutes, whisking constantly. Remove from the heat, discard the bay leaf, and stir in the grated cheese. Season to taste.

Assemble the lasagne in layers in a baking dish. Start with one-third of the meat sauce, then add one-third of the spinach, two sheets of lasagne, and one-third of the cheese sauce. Repeat these layers twice, then top with the grated cheese. Bake for 35–40 minutes. Leave to rest in a warm place for 10 minutes before serving.

LAMB

New-season British lamb is unbeatable in the spring. At other times of the year, chilled fresh New Zealand lamb is inexpensive and good, so don't overlook it. Welsh salt-marsh lamb is available from June to October, and well worth buying for its unique flavour and tenderness. Deeper red than other lamb, it tastes like it's been pre-seasoned. This is its natural flavour, which comes from the grasses and sea plants on which the lambs graze.

2 French-trimmed racks of lamb (best end),
    each with 6 bones, outer layer of fat removed
2tbsp fennel seeds
1tbsp cumin seeds
1tsp coarsely ground black pepper
100g natural yogurt
Leaves picked from 1 small bunch of fresh mint
Leaves picked from 1 small bunch of fresh coriander
SERVES THREE Olive oil, for drizzling

LAMB CUTLETS INDIAN STYLE

Get your butcher to cut each rack into three double cutlets, each with two bones, then to remove one bone from each of the double cutlets.

Toast the fennel seeds, cumin seeds, and black pepper in a dry frying pan over a low to medium heat for a few minutes until fragrant, then blitz in a blender with the yogurt and herbs to make a thick paste. Put the cutlets in a dish and smother with the yogurt mixture. Cover and leave to marinate in the fridge overnight.

The next day, heat the oven to 160°C fan (180°C/gas 4).

Heat a griddle pan until hot. Sear the cutlets over a medium to high heat for about 10 minutes, drizzling them with olive oil and turning them over once. Transfer the cutlets to a roasting pan, cover with foil, and place in the oven to roast for 20–25 minutes. Leave to rest in a warm place for about 5 minutes before serving.

1tsp ground coriander
1tsp ground cumin
1tsp coarsely ground black pepper
500g minced lamb
1 onion, finely chopped
2 garlic cloves, crushed
Leaves picked from 1 bunch of fresh
    flat-leaf parsley, finely chopped
Leaves picked from 1 bunch of
    fresh mint, finely chopped
3tbsp soy sauce
1tbsp sweet chilli sauce
½tsp fine salt
Vegetable oil

FOR THE RAITA
1tbsp cumin seeds
½ cucumber
200g natural yogurt
Sea salt and freshly milled
    black pepper

SPICY LAMB STICKS WITH RAITA

First make the raita. Toast the cumin seeds in a dry frying pan over a low to medium heat for a few minutes until fragrant. Remove and crush lightly with a pestle or the end of a rolling pin. Peel the cucumber, then halve lengthways and scrape out the seeds. Grate the cucumber flesh on to kitchen paper. Wrap and squeeze out the excess moisture. Combine the cumin and cucumber with the yogurt in a bowl and add seasoning to taste. Cover and keep in the fridge until serving time.

For the lamb sticks, toast the ground coriander, cumin, and pepper as for the cumin seeds above, then tip into a bowl. Add all the other ingredients except the oil. Using your hands, squeeze the mixture well to bind it together. Divide among 12 skewers, shaping and squeezing the mixture firmly around them. Place on a tray.

Heat a large griddle pan over a medium heat until hot. Brush the lamb sticks with oil, then cook for 12–15 minutes until golden brown on all sides, turning them frequently. Leave to rest in a warm place for 5 minutes before serving with the raita.

As an alternative…shape the lamb around wooden cocktail sticks and serve as canapés. They will only need to be cooked for 4–5 minutes.

Leaves picked from 1 bunch of fresh rosemary
12 garlic cloves, peeled and quartered
4tbsp light olive oil
15g sea or rock salt
1 shoulder of lamb on the bone, weighing about 2kg
Jersey Royal potatoes, cooked and tossed in butter
and sea salt, to serve

FOR THE VEGETABLES
7tbsp light olive oil
1–2 bunches of spring carrots, peeled and halved lengthways
A few sprigs each of fresh rosemary and thyme
2–3 heads of garlic, each cut crossways in half
500g shelled fresh or frozen peas
Leaves picked from 1 small bunch of fresh mint, shredded
Sea salt and freshly milled black pepper

SERVES SIX

SLOW-ROAST SHOULDER OF LAMB WITH SPRING VEGETABLES

Heat the oven to 140°C fan (160°C/gas 3).

Put the rosemary and garlic in a blender with the olive oil and salt, and blitz until well chopped. Using your hands, massage the mix all over the lamb in a roasting pan. Cover with foil and roast for 2 hours. Remove from the oven and leave the lamb to rest while you cook the vegetables and garlic.

Heat 4tbsp of the olive oil in a frying pan over a medium heat. Add the carrots, rosemary, thyme, and some seasoning, and fry for about 15 minutes until the carrots are tender, tossing them frequently.

Meanwhile, in a separate frying pan, cook the garlic, cut-side down, in 1tbsp hot olive oil for about 5 minutes until golden brown. Cook the peas in a pan of boiling salted water for 3 minutes until tender; drain and crush lightly with the mint and about 2tbsp olive oil.

Carve the lamb and serve with the garlic, carrots, peas, and potatoes.

The cooking time is for rare meat...but if you prefer your lamb cooked more than this, increase the time. An extra 15 minutes will give medium-rare meat.

2 fillets of lamb, from the middle neck
Vegetable oil
1 large baguette, halved lengthways
Sea salt and freshly milled black pepper

FOR THE MINT SAUCE
50g caster sugar
50ml white wine vinegar

SERVES FOUR   Leaves picked from 1 large bunch of fresh mint

LAMB BAGUETTE
WITH FRESH
MINT SAUCE

First make the mint sauce. Dissolve the sugar in the wine vinegar
in a small pan over a low heat, then bring to the boil and boil for
5 minutes. Leave to cool for 10 minutes. Add the mint leaves and
blitz with a hand blender until roughly chopped. Set aside.

Cut the lamb into 1cm-thick slices on the diagonal. Season well.
Heat some oil in a frying pan over a medium to high heat and cook
the lamb slices for 5–8 minutes until well seared on both sides.

Meanwhile, get the grill hot.

Remove the lamb from the pan (reserve the pan juices) and leave
to rest in a warm place for 5 minutes while you toast the cut sides
of the baguette under the grill.

Place the lamb slices over one half of the baguette. Drizzle with
the pan juices and mint sauce, then top with the other half of the
baguette. Cut into quarters and serve.

Leftover roast lamb...is also good served this way.
Slice it as for the fresh lamb and use cold, or wrap
the slices in foil and reheat in the oven at 170°C fan
(190°C/gas 5) for 10 minutes.

PORK

Loin of pork used to be the top joint for roasting, but now we know that the belly, shoulder, and leg are the best. The reason is their fat content, which makes them virtually self-basting and gives them flavour and succulence. Loin joints are too lean to roast, although loin chops can be good. The secret lies in not overcooking them. Well-done pork is dry and tough, and a thing of the past.

1 boned shoulder of pork, weighing
about 1.5kg, rind scored
Vegetable oil
Sea salt and freshly milled black pepper

FOR THE STUFFING
200g pork sausagemeat
100g fresh breadcrumbs
2tsp chopped fresh sage
1 onion, very finely diced
Finely grated zest of 2 lemons
2tbsp melted butter
1 medium organic egg, beaten
½tsp fine salt

SERVES SIX

ROAST PORK WITH SAGE, ONION, AND LEMON STUFFING

Heat the oven to 160°C fan (180°C/gas 4).

Lay the pork flat, rind-side down, on a board. Combine the stuffing ingredients together and place in a line down the centre of the pork. Roll the meat around the stuffing and tie at regular intervals with string. Rub the joint all over with oil, salt, and pepper.

Place the pork in a roasting pan and roast for about 2 hours until the juices run clear when a skewer is inserted in the centre. Allow to rest for about 10 minutes before carving.

If the joint is difficult to roll...cut away a little of the meat inside to create a pocket for the stuffing. If you still can't get all the stuffing in, put the remainder in a baking dish and bake alongside the joint for 45 minutes.

4 pork loin chops
Light olive oil
A few sprigs of fresh thyme
2 Romaine or Cos lettuces, halved lengthways
A few bay leaves
A few sprigs of fresh rosemary
300ml hot chicken stock

FOR THE MARINADE
40g fresh root ginger, peeled and finely grated
2 stalks lemongrass, finely chopped
3tbsp hoisin sauce
2tbsp toasted sesame oil

SERVES FOUR

ASIAN PORK CHOPS WITH SEARED LETTUCE

Mix all the marinade ingredients together and spread evenly over both sides of the chops. Place in a dish, cover, and refrigerate for a minimum of 4 hours, or overnight.

Heat the oven to 160°C fan (180°C/gas 4).

Warm a little olive oil in a large frying pan over a medium to high heat. Add the chops with a few thyme sprigs and sear until they are well coloured on both sides. Remove and set aside.

Heat a dry griddle pan over a medium to high heat until hot. Brush the cut sides of the lettuces with oil, then place, cut-side down, in the pan and sear until golden brown. Transfer the lettuce, seared-side up, to a large baking dish. Sprinkle with the bay and rosemary. Place the chops on top. Spread them with any marinade left in the dish and pour over the stock.

Cover with foil and bake for 15 minutes. Remove the foil and baste the chops with the juices in the dish, then continue cooking uncovered for about 10 minutes. At the end of cooking, the chops should be tender when pierced with a fork in their thickest part. Leave to rest in a warm place for 5 minutes before serving.

1 piece of boned pork belly, weighing
about 2kg, rind scored
Vegetable oil

Sea salt and freshly milled black pepper

BARBECUED
BELLY OF PORK

Light the barbecue. When the flames have died down, the coals
are white, and the temperature is medium, you're ready to cook.

Rub the pork all over with oil and seasoning, then place on the
grid of the barbecue. Cook for about 3 hours, turning the meat over
from time to time. Try to keep the heat at an even temperature during
cooking, and take care not to let the meat get too darkly coloured or
charred on the outside – you may need to move the grid farther away
from the heat, or push the meat to the edges of the grid, or even lift
the meat off for a few minutes if the heat gets too intense.

Leave the pork to rest in a warm place for 10 minutes before
slicing into thick rashers for serving.

When barbecuing pork...it's important that the meat
is cooked right through to the centre. With the long
cooking time in this recipe, you'll need to replenish
the coals to keep the heat constant.

CHICKEN

How can anyone not like chicken? It's such a versatile, everyday meat, and such an easy source of protein. Take the chicken breast – what could be quicker and more simple to prepare? Cut it in half and open it out, then season and griddle with the skin on for 4–5 minutes each side. As for a whole chicken for roasting, you get what you pay for, and nothing beats the golden colour and rich flavour of an organic, corn-fed bird.

1 large bunch of fresh thyme
1 large bunch of fresh rosemary
1 large organic chicken, preferably corn fed,
    weighing about 1.8kg
1 head of garlic, cut crossways in half
40 garlic cloves, unpeeled
A few bay leaves
Olive oil
2 baby Little Gem lettuces, halved lengthways
200ml hot chicken stock

SERVES FOUR Sea salt and freshly milled black pepper

ROAST CHICKEN WITH FORTY CLOVES OF GARLIC

Heat the oven to 160°C fan (180°C/gas 4).

Push half of the thyme and rosemary sprigs inside the cavity of the chicken, then put the chicken in a roasting dish. Surround with all of the garlic, the bay leaves, and remaining thyme and rosemary. Drizzle olive oil over the chicken and season well. Roast for 1 hour.

Add the lettuces and stock to the dish and baste the chicken well, then roast for another hour. Cover with foil and leave to rest in a warm place for 15 minutes before carving.

4 skinless, boneless organic chicken breasts
8 back bacon rashers, any rind removed
2tbsp vegetable oil

FOR THE PESTO
Leaves picked from 1 large bunch of fresh basil
50g pine nuts, toasted
1 small garlic clove, crushed
50g Parmesan cheese, freshly grated
50ml olive oil
Sea salt and freshly milled black pepper

SERVES FOUR

CHICKEN
WITH BACON
AND PESTO

Make the pesto by blitzing the basil leaves in a blender with the pine nuts, garlic, grated Parmesan, and olive oil until almost smooth. Season to taste and set aside.

Heat the oven to 180°C fan (200°C/gas 6).

Create a pocket in each chicken breast by making a cut in one side. Spoon one-quarter of the pesto into each pocket and bring the open edges together. Wrap each breast tightly with two bacon rashers.

Heat the oil in an ovenproof frying pan over a high heat. Place the chicken breasts in the pan and brown well on both sides. Transfer the pan to the oven and roast for 10 minutes, turning the chicken once or twice. Remove from the oven and leave to rest in a warm place for about 5 minutes, then slice each breast diagonally in half. Serve hot, drizzled with the pan juices.

Vegetable oil
400ml can coconut milk
2 carrots, peeled and cut into chunks on the diagonal
250g tenderstem broccoli
200g mangetout, halved on the diagonal
6 skinless, boneless organic chicken thighs
150g beansprouts
Leaves picked from 1 small bunch of fresh coriander, chopped
Sea salt

FOR THE SPICE PASTE
2 green chillies, roughly chopped with the seeds
1 stalk lemongrass, thinly sliced
1 bunch of fresh coriander
80g fresh root ginger, peeled and chopped
2 garlic cloves, quartered
1 onion, cut into eighths
5tbsp fish sauce
50g caster sugar
1tsp fine salt

SERVES FOUR

THAI GREEN
CHICKEN CURRY

Blitz the spice paste ingredients to a chunky purée in a blender or food processor. Heat a little oil in a large frying pan and stir-fry the paste for 5 minutes. Pour in 200ml cold water, stir, and bring to the boil. Simmer for 15 minutes. Stir in the coconut milk and bring back to the boil, then strain into a clean, large pan. Bring to a gentle simmer and taste for seasoning – you may want to add more fish sauce, sugar, or salt. Keep the pan of sauce over a low heat.

Bring a large pan of salted water to the boil. Blanch the vegetables separately – boil the carrots for 3 minutes, the broccoli for 2 minutes, and the mangetout for 1 minute. As each is blanched, remove with a slotted spoon and refresh under the cold tap. Set aside.

Heat a little oil in a frying pan over a medium to high heat and sear the chicken for about 10 minutes until golden brown on all sides. Add to the sauce and simmer for about 10 minutes until almost tender. Add the blanched vegetables and simmer for a further 4 minutes.

Meanwhile, toss the beansprouts briefly in a dry frying pan over a medium heat until hot. Add the chopped coriander, sprinkle with oil and sea salt, and toss to mix.

Remove the chicken from the sauce and slice into bite-sized strips on the diagonal. Serve the vegetables and chicken topped with the hot beansprouts, with the sauce spooned over and around.

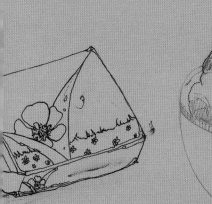

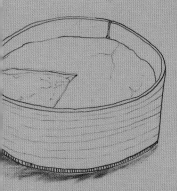
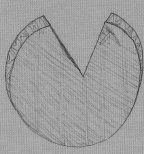

DAIRY & EGGS

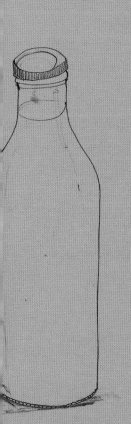

CHEESE

For me, mature Cheddar is one of the best English cheeses. It's great for cooking because it has a powerful flavour and melts beautifully. Cheddar is easy to keep and consistently good, unlike soft cheeses, which need the right temperature to achieve perfect ripeness – virtually impossible at home. Goat's cheese is another good cheese for melting. Softer and creamier than Cheddar, it softens well but still keeps its shape when warm.

125g cold unsalted butter, diced
250g plain white flour
80g mature Cheddar cheese, grated
½tsp black peppercorns, finely crushed
Sea salt
MAKES FIFTEEN A little milk

CHEESE STRAWS

Heat the oven to 190°C fan (210°C/gas 6½). Line a baking tray with non-stick baking parchment.

Rub the butter into the flour with your fingertips until the mixture resembles breadcrumbs. Stir in 60g of the cheese, the crushed black pepper, and 1tsp sea salt, then bind with just enough milk (about 1tbsp) to make a firm dough.

Roll out the dough on a floured surface until 1cm thick. Cut into about 15 strips that are 20cm long and 1cm wide. Lay the strips on the baking tray and brush with milk, then sprinkle with the remaining cheese and sea salt to taste. Bake for 15 minutes until golden and crisp. Cool on the baking tray before serving.

25g unsalted butter
2 onions, sliced
Leaves picked from 1 small bunch of fresh thyme
100g mature Cheddar cheese, grated
150g sliced cooked ham, cut into small pieces
2tbsp Branston pickle
Sea salt and freshly milled black pepper

FOR THE PASTRY
100g cold unsalted butter, diced
225g plain white flour
1 medium organic egg, beaten
A little milk

MAKES FIVE

CHEESE, HAM AND PICKLE PASTIES

First make the pastry. Rub the butter into the flour with your fingertips until the mixture resembles breadcrumbs. Add the egg and mix well, then mix in just enough milk to make a firm dough. Wrap in cling film and leave to rest in the fridge while you prepare the filling.

Melt the butter in a moderately hot pan. Add the onions and thyme and cook, stirring regularly, until the onions break down and turn a dark golden colour. This should take about 20 minutes. Season well, then leave to cool.

Divide the pastry into five equal pieces and roll out each piece into a 15cm disc. Stack the discs between non-stick baking parchment and keep in the fridge until you're ready to use them.

Heat the oven to 180°C fan (200°C/gas 6). Line a baking tray with non-stick baking parchment.

Mix the cheese, ham, and pickle into the cooled onions. Lay the pastry discs out and divide the filling equally among them, spreading it in an even layer and leaving a border clear around the edge. Brush the edge of each disc with milk, then fold over and press to seal.

Sit the pasties up on the baking tray so the seams are running down the centre. Neatly flute the seams, then brush the pasties all over with milk. Bake for 15 minutes until golden. Serve hot or cold.

100g wheel of goat's cheese
25g walnuts
50g dried figs, chopped
3tbsp balsamic vinegar

1tbsp clear honey

BAKED GOAT'S CHEESE WITH FIGS AND WALNUTS

Heat the oven to 180°C fan (200°C/gas 6).

Lay the wheel of cheese in a baking dish and bake for 10 minutes. Meanwhile, spread the walnuts out on a baking tray and toast in the oven for 5 minutes, then chop roughly.

Place the figs in a small pan with the vinegar, and toss over a medium to high heat for 1–2 minutes until reduced and syrupy.

Serve the goat's cheese topped with the figs and walnuts, and drizzled with the honey.

250g log of goat's cheese, sliced into discs
250g lightly pickled or mildly malted baby
    beetroot, halved
150g rocket
Extra virgin olive oil
Sea salt and freshly milled black pepper

FOR THE PRALINE
75g hazelnuts
Light olive oil
60g caster sugar
SERVES FOUR   Pinch of fine salt

GOAT'S CHEESE AND BEETROOT SALAD WITH PRALINE

Heat the oven to 180°C fan (200°C/gas 6).

First make the praline. Toast the hazelnuts on a baking tray in the oven for 6–8 minutes. Tip into a bowl and set aside. Brush the tray with olive oil and reserve. Melt the sugar with 1½tbsp water in a small frying pan over a low heat. When melted, bring to the boil and simmer for a few minutes until it turns to a golden caramel, swirling the caramel in the pan occasionally (don't stir). Add the hazelnuts and salt and mix well. Pour on to the oiled tray in a small pool and leave to cool.

When the praline is cold and set, remove it from the tray and chop roughly with a sharp knife.

Arrange the cheese, beetroot, and rocket in a serving bowl. Drizzle with olive oil, then sprinkle over the praline and some salt and pepper.

CREAM

Double and whipping cream are interchangeable in most recipes, although there's quite a difference between the two of them – double cream contains 48–54 per cent fat, whipping cream only 35–40 per cent. Whipping cream is the more stable of the two in cooking, because the extra fat content of double cream makes it more likely to split, but the beauty of double cream is that you only need a small quantity to add instant richness to a dish.

250ml double or whipping cream
4tbsp clear honey
500g natural yogurt
200–250g mini marshmallows

SERVES SIX   300g raspberries

AMBROSIA

Whip the cream in a large bowl until it will just hold its shape. Warm the honey in the microwave, or in a small pan on top of the stove, to liquefy it, then whisk into the yogurt until evenly incorporated. Fold the cream into the yogurt until well combined, then gently fold in the marshmallows and 250g of the raspberries.

Cover and refrigerate for at least 4 hours. Serve chilled, with the remaining raspberries scattered on top.

Mini marshmallows...are the perfect size for this dish. If you can only get large marshmallows, snip them in half with kitchen scissors.

375ml whipping or double cream
200ml milk
20g fresh basil, chopped (including the stalks)
75g caster sugar
8 medium organic egg yolks
Demerara sugar, for sprinkling

BASIL CRÈME BRÛLÉE

Bring the cream, milk, and basil to the boil in a pan, then remove from the heat. Whisk the sugar with the egg yolks in a bowl. Add a little hot cream and mix well. Pour this mixture into the pan and stir well, then pour back into the bowl. Leave to infuse for 30 minutes. Strain the custard mixture into a jug.

Heat the oven to 130°C fan (150°C/gas 2). Place eight 125ml ramekins in a roasting pan.

Divide the custard evenly among the ramekins. Pour boiling water into the roasting pan to come halfway up the sides of the ramekins. Cover the whole pan with foil and place carefully in the oven. Bake for 40–50 minutes – the custards are done when there is still a slight wobble in the centre; if necessary, cook for a few minutes longer. Remove the ramekins from the pan of water and leave to cool for about an hour, then refrigerate for at least 2–3 hours.

To serve, sprinkle liberally with Demerara sugar and glaze with a blowtorch until the sugar caramelizes.

Basil is best...in the summer. In winter, flavour the custard with 3 broken cinnamon sticks.

200g full-fat soft cheese
60g caster sugar
400g crème fraîche
1 lemon
3 leaves gelatine
4tbsp milk

FOR THE BASE
200g gingernut biscuits

40g unsalted butter, melted

CRÈME FRAÎCHE CHEESECAKE

To make the base, crush the gingernuts in a plastic bag with a rolling pin. Tip into a bowl and mix in the melted butter. Press firmly over the bottom of a 20cm springform tin or deep, loose-bottomed cake tin. Refrigerate while you prepare the filling.

Whisk the cheese and sugar together in a large bowl until smooth. Add the crème fraîche and mix until smooth. Finely grate the zest from the lemon, then halve the lemon and squeeze the juice from one half. Stir the zest and juice into the cream mix until evenly combined.

Soak the gelatine in a bowl of cold water for 5 minutes. Heat the milk in a small pan until almost boiling, then remove from the heat. Lift the gelatine from the soaking water and squeeze dry, then drop into the hot milk and stir until melted.

Transfer about one-quarter of the cream mix to a medium bowl. Strain in the gelatine milk while whisking, then return this to the rest of the cream mix and combine thoroughly. Pour the cream filling into the tin. Tap it gently on the work surface to smooth out and remove any air bubbles. Refrigerate for 1½–2 hours until set.

To serve, run a hot knife around the rim of the cheesecake, then release the spring and remove the side of the tin. Using a palette knife, release the biscuit base from the base of the tin and slide the cheesecake on to a plate. Serve chilled.

EGGS

With eggs, the fresher they are the better. Very fresh eggs will help cakes rise, and make custards set more quickly. When whipping the whites, the freshest eggs will give the greatest volume. To check for freshness, crack an egg on to a plate: the white should cling to the yolk, which should look domed, not flat. Organic eggs are my choice – they have deep-coloured yolks and a rich flavour.

9 large organic egg yolks
90g caster sugar
600ml whipping or double cream
1 whole nutmeg, for grating

SERVES FOUR

BAKED EGG CUSTARD

Heat the oven to 130°C fan (150°C/gas 2).

Whisk the egg yolks and sugar in a bowl until combined. Bring the cream just to the boil in a pan, then whisk into the egg yolks. Strain through a fine sieve into a 1-litre baking dish. Grate nutmeg liberally over the top to cover it completely.

Bake for 25–35 minutes until the custard is just set – it should still have a slight wobble in the centre when you gently shake the dish. Leave to stand at room temperature for 20 minutes before serving, or cool completely and then serve chilled.

1 medium organic egg, in its shell
200ml extra virgin olive oil
Fine salt
About 20 young asparagus spears,

          trimmed if necessary

MOUSSELINE
WITH ASPARAGUS

Bring a small pan of water to the boil. Place the egg in the water and boil for 5 minutes, then lift out and cool under the cold tap. Peel the egg, place it in a bowl, and break it up with a hand blender (it will be very liquid in the centre).

Add the olive oil slowly – in a very thin drizzle – blending it in well after each addition until the mousseline is thick and smooth. Add salt to taste. Transfer to a bowl, cover, and refrigerate until ready to serve.

Bring a large pan of salted water to the boil. Add the asparagus and simmer for 2–3 minutes until just tender. Remove and refresh under the cold tap.

Serve the asparagus dipped into the chilled mousseline.

350g icing sugar
200g ground almonds
40g plain white flour
7 medium organic egg whites
90g caster sugar
1 vanilla pod, split lengthways, or a few drops of vanilla extract
100g white chocolate, melted and cooled

MAKES
TWENTY-FIVE

MACAROONS

Line three heavy baking trays with non-stick baking parchment. Have ready a piping bag fitted with a plain nozzle, or a strong plastic bag with a small hole cut diagonally across one corner.

Sift the icing sugar, almonds, and flour into a bowl; set aside. Whisk the egg whites to stiff peaks in an electric mixer on full speed. Add the caster sugar and continue to whisk for 4 minutes. Scrape in the seeds from the vanilla pod, or add the vanilla extract, and whisk briefly.

Using a rubber spatula, mix in one-third of the dry ingredients, then add the remaining dry ingredients and fold in with the spatula until just combined.

Spoon the mixture into the piping bag. Pipe a few small dots under the parchment lining on the baking trays so the paper will stick to the trays. Now pipe 50 discs on the parchment, each one about 3.5cm in diameter, spacing them evenly. When you finish each tray, pick it up and tap its base gently on the work surface to spread the discs a little.

Leave the trays in a warm, dry place for 15–20 minutes so the macaroons can dry out a bit – you should be able to gently run your fingertip across the top of a disc without it sticking. Meanwhile, heat the oven to 110°C fan (130°C/gas ½).

Bake the macaroons for 20 minutes until they can be peeled off the parchment without sticking. Allow to cool on the trays, then sandwich together in pairs with melted white chocolate in between.

To make pink macaroons...use a drop or two of red food colouring instead of vanilla, and fill with strawberry or raspberry jam instead of chocolate.

FRUIT

APPLES

It's important to choose the correct variety of apple for the dish you're making. An apple's sweetness and texture vary according to its sugar and water content, which is why you should use what the recipe says. I also recommend that you try to buy locally grown fruit – English apples are the best in the world. The one exception is the Braeburn apple from New Zealand, an eater that doubles as a cooker with exceptionally good results.

FOR THE GRANITA
40g caster sugar
600g Granny Smith apples
A generous pinch of ascorbic
    acid powder (vitamin C)
Juice of ½ lime

FOR THE JELLY
4 leaves gelatine
100ml clear honey
300ml sweet white wine
    (Sauternes or Muscat)

TO SERVE
200g natural Greek yogurt
2tsp caster sugar, or to taste

SERVES SIX

APPLE GRANITA WITH WINE JELLY

First make the granita. Dissolve the sugar in 2½tbsp water in a pan and bring to the boil. Remove from the heat and leave to cool.

Roughly chop the apples, discarding the cores, and toss them with the ascorbic acid to prevent browning. Juice the apples using an electric juicer (or core the apples and then purée in a blender with 100ml water). Add the lime juice to the apple juice, then strain through a fine sieve into a bowl. Stir in the sugar syrup.

Freeze in a large plastic tray until frozen. This should take about 4 hours. Whisk the granita well after the first hour to prevent large ice crystals from forming. When fully frozen, scrape the granita into a slush with a fork. Keep in a rigid container in the freezer for up to 1 week.

To make the jelly, soak the gelatine in cold water for 5 minutes. Warm the honey in a pan over a medium heat and let it bubble for 3 minutes. Drain the gelatine and squeeze dry, then add to the honey with the wine. Stir over the heat for 2 minutes until the gelatine has melted. Strain into six small glasses (about 150ml) and cool. Refrigerate for 2 hours until set.

To serve, sweeten the yogurt with sugar to taste, then spoon over the jelly and top with the granita.

3 Granny Smith apples,
    about 375g total weight
1tsp ground cinnamon
1tsp ground mixed spice
1tsp ground ginger
175g caster sugar
350g self-raising white flour
125g unsalted butter, diced
2 medium organic eggs,
    beaten
125ml milk

FOR THE CRUMBLE TOPPING
50g ground almonds
25g caster sugar
25g plain white flour
2tsp ground cinnamon
1tsp ground mixed spice
1tsp ground ginger
25g unsalted butter, melted

**CUTS INTO
TEN SLICES**

SPICED APPLE
CRUMBLE CAKE

Heat the oven to 170°C fan (190°C/gas 5). Grease a 24cm non-stick springform cake tin.

First make the crumble topping. Put all the ingredients, except the butter, in a bowl and mix well. Stir in the butter. Set aside.

Peel, quarter, and core the apples, then slice thinly. Combine the spices and 50g of the sugar in a bowl, add the apple slices, and toss to coat. Mix the flour and remaining 125g sugar in a separate large bowl. Rub in the butter until the mixture resembles breadcrumbs. Add the eggs and milk, and mix until just combined. Gently fold in the apples. Spoon the mixture into the cake tin and level the surface.

Sprinkle the crumble topping over the cake and press gently with your fingers so that some sinks down into the cake mixture. Bake for 30–35 minutes until a skewer inserted in the centre comes out clean. Cool in the tin before serving.

4 Bramley apples, about 1kg total weight
60g unsalted butter
2 cinnamon sticks, each broken in half
About 50g caster sugar

MAKES 500ML

APPLE PURÉE

Peel, quarter, and core the apples, then slice thinly. Heat the butter with the cinnamon sticks in a large pan until the butter begins to foam, then add the apples and sugar. Cook over a medium heat for about 15 minutes until the apples have broken up, stirring frequently so they don't catch on the bottom of the pan.

Remove the cinnamon, and purée the apples in a blender until smooth. Taste for sweetness and add more sugar if you like. Push the purée through a fine sieve into a bowl. Cover and keep in the fridge.

Serve hot or cold with pork or duck...or increase the sugar to 150g and use as a dessert with ice cream or cream, or as a pie or tart filling.

BANANAS

As bananas ripen, their starch converts to sugar and their flavour and sweetness increase, so for baking you must choose the brownest, most overripe bananas you can find. If there are bananas in the fruit bowl that are past their best for eating, then these are ideal. If you haven't time for baking, wrap the bananas well and freeze them. They'll keep for months.

80g caster sugar
2 very ripe or overripe bananas, peeled
    and mashed to a smooth purée
200ml milk
375ml whipping or double cream
5 medium organic egg yolks
4 leaves gelatine
25ml dark rum

SERVES SIX   Vanilla ice cream and melted dark chocolate, to serve

BANANA CARAMEL BAVAROIS

Heat a heavy frying pan over a high heat until hot. Add the sugar and spread evenly, then leave without stirring over a low to medium heat until melted to a very light golden caramel. This should take 5–8 minutes. Before the caramel gets too dark, beat in the bananas until smooth, then mix in the milk and 75ml of the cream. Remove from the heat.

Whisk a little of the creamy mix into the egg yolks in a bowl. Pour this mixture back into the pan and combine thoroughly with a wooden spatula. Stir over a low heat until the banana custard is thick enough to coat the back of the spatula. Transfer to a bowl.

Soak the gelatine in a bowl of cold water for 5 minutes. Lift out and squeeze to remove excess moisture, then drop into the hot banana custard and stir until melted. Stir in the rum. Lay cling film on the surface of the custard to prevent a skin from forming, then refrigerate.

When the custard is almost cool, beat it until smooth. Whip the remaining cream to soft peaks and fold into the custard until evenly incorporated. Divide the mix among six glasses or dishes, cover, and refrigerate for 1–2 hours until firm.

To serve, top with small quenelles or scoops of ice cream and drizzle with melted chocolate.

75g panko (Japanese) breadcrumbs
1tsp ground cinnamon
25g plain white flour
2 medium organic egg whites
2 ripe but firm bananas
Vegetable oil, for deep-frying
Caster sugar, to finish

FOR THE SPICED CREAM
100g crème fraîche
Finely grated zest of 1 lemon
½tsp ground mixed spice

SERVES TWO

BANANA FRITTERS WITH SPICED CREAM

Make the spiced cream by mixing all the ingredients together. Keep in the fridge until needed.

Toss the breadcrumbs with the cinnamon in a bowl. Put the flour and egg whites in two other bowls; lightly beat the whites to loosen and mix them. Peel the bananas and cut each one crossways into three equal pieces, discarding the pointed ends.

Dip the banana pieces first in the flour, then in the egg whites, and finally in the breadcrumbs, coating them evenly. Shake off any excess coating, then repeat the dipping with the egg whites and crumbs. Set aside in the fridge until ready to cook.

Heat vegetable oil in a deep-fat fryer to 165°C. Deep-fry the banana fritters, in batches, for a few minutes until golden and crisp. Lift them out and drain on kitchen paper. Sprinkle with caster sugar and serve immediately, with the spiced cream.

150g soft unsalted butter
150g Demerara sugar
3 medium eggs, beaten
2 very ripe or overripe bananas,
   peeled and mashed
150g plain white flour
1tsp baking powder

FOR THE TOFFEE SAUCE
50g unsalted butter, diced
50g Demerara sugar
3tbsp golden syrup
125ml whipping or double cream

SERVES SIX

BAKED BANANA PUDDINGS

Heat the oven to 180°C fan (200°C/gas 6). Grease six individual 200ml pudding moulds.

First make the sauce. Melt the butter in a pan with the sugar, stirring until the sugar dissolves. Add the golden syrup and cream and simmer gently, stirring, for 1 minute. Remove from the heat.

For the puddings, cream the butter and sugar in a bowl until fluffy. Add the eggs and bananas and beat well to mix. Sift the flour and baking powder together, and fold into the creamed mixture until evenly incorporated.

Put 1tbsp toffee sauce in the bottom of each mould, then divide half of the pudding mix among them. Repeat the layers, then finish with a layer of toffee sauce. Bake for 20–25 minutes until the puddings are golden and spring back when lightly pressed. Remove from the oven and leave to rest for a few minutes, then turn out and serve warm.

To make a large pudding...use a 1.5-litre pudding basin with three equal layers of toffee sauce and two of pudding mix. Bake for 50–60 minutes.

BERRIES

Seasonality counts for everything with berries, so shun imports and wait for British berries as they come into season in the summer. Only then are they ripe and juicy, and full of sweetness and flavour. Buy in small quantities, choosing the darkest, plumpest berries you can find. Wrap the punnets in bags and keep them in the fridge until you are ready to use them.

1 large punnet of strawberries (about 400g),
   hulled and quartered
3tbsp extra virgin olive oil
2tbsp aged balsamic vinegar
4 small meringues (nests or shells),
   lightly crushed
About 5tbsp clotted cream

SERVES FOUR   A few fresh basil leaves, finely shredded

BALSAMIC STRAWBERRIES WITH MERINGUE

Place the strawberries in a large bowl. Mix the olive oil and balsamic vinegar together in a jug, then add enough to the strawberries to coat them lightly. Arrange the fruit on a serving plate and place the pieces of meringue among them. Top with quenelles or spoonfuls of clotted cream and the shredded basil. Drizzle the remaining dressing around the edge. Serve straightaway.

Instead of aged balsamic vinegar...you can substitute 60ml ordinary balsamic vinegar boiled until reduced by half. Cool before using.

4 leaves gelatine
400g can blackberries or
    summer fruits
100g caster sugar
100ml crème de mûre
    (blackberry liqueur) or
    your favourite fruit liqueur
175g sponge fingers
1 large punnet of blackberries
    (about 300g)

FOR THE CUSTARD
4 leaves gelatine
250ml milk
250ml whipping or double cream
1 vanilla pod, split lengthways
5 medium organic egg yolks
75g caster sugar

TO FINISH
75g crème fraîche
80g mascarpone
30g caster sugar

SERVES SIX

BLACKBERRY
TRIFLE

Put 4 leaves of gelatine to soak in a bowl of cold water. Meanwhile, blitz the canned blackberries with their juice in a blender until smooth, then pass through a fine sieve into a pan. Dissolve the sugar in the blackberry liquid over a low heat and bring to the boil. Lift the gelatine out of the water and squeeze to remove excess moisture, then drop into the pan and stir until melted. Add the liqueur. Set the jelly mix aside.

Break the sponge fingers into 2cm pieces. Combine with the fresh blackberries in a serving bowl. Pour over the jelly mix and chill in the fridge until almost set.

Meanwhile, make the custard. Put the 4 leaves of gelatine to soak in a bowl of cold water. Combine the milk, cream, and vanilla pod in a pan and bring to the boil. Whisk the egg yolks with the sugar in a bowl until smooth, then whisk in a little of the hot cream mixture. Pour into the pan and mix thoroughly with a wooden spatula. Stir over a low heat until the custard is thick enough to coat the spatula. Remove from the heat.

Lift the gelatine out of the water and squeeze to remove excess moisture, then add to the custard and stir until melted. Pour through a fine sieve into a clean bowl. Lay a piece of cling film on the surface to prevent a skin from forming, then place in the fridge. When the custard is cold, give it a good whisk and spoon on top of the blackberry jelly.

To finish, whisk the crème fraîche, mascarpone, and sugar together, and spread over the custard. Chill for at least an hour before serving.

For a finishing touch...sprinkle the trifle with crushed praline just before serving. A recipe for praline is on page 118.

200g white chocolate
325ml whipping or double cream
1 large punnet of raspberries (about 250g)
100ml crème de framboise (raspberry liqueur)

SERVES SIX

RASPBERRIES WITH WHITE CHOCOLATE MOUSSE

Roughly chop the chocolate and put into a large bowl. Bring 200ml of the cream just to the boil in a small pan and pour over the chocolate. Leave to stand for 5 minutes, then whisk until smooth. Lay a piece of cling film on the surface of the chocolate mixture to prevent a skin from forming, and set aside to cool.

Whip the remaining cream to soft peaks, then fold into the cooled chocolate mixture in two batches until smooth. Cover with cling film as before and refrigerate for a minimum of 2 hours. Meanwhile, gently combine the raspberries and raspberry liqueur in another bowl, cover, and set aside.

To serve, scoop the chocolate mousse with a hot spoon on to serving plates. Arrange the raspberries to the side and drizzle with a little of the raspberry liqueur.

LEMONS AND LIMES

For juiciness, buy unwaxed lemons with thin skins. Some specialist shops sell Sicilian lemons with their stalks and leaves intact. Ripened under the hot Italian sun, these are well worth the extra you'll pay for them. Limes are less harsh in flavour than lemons, but they can be hard and dry with hardly any juice. The best way to check is to give them a quick squeeze. A juicy, ripe lime will feel soft and give a little under pressure.

FOR THE FILLING
396g can condensed milk
Juice of 4 large lemons (about 200ml)
4 medium organic egg yolks
125g caster sugar

150g soft unsalted butter
125g caster sugar
1 medium organic egg,
        beaten

FOR THE TOPPING
3 medium organic egg whites
150g caster sugar

CUTS INTO
TEN SLICES
250g plain white flour
1tsp baking powder

LEMON MERINGUE SLICE

Heat the oven to 180°C fan (200°C/gas 6). Grease a 30 x 20 x 5cm baking tin and line with non-stick baking parchment.

Cream the butter with the sugar in a bowl until fluffy. Beat in the egg, then fold in the flour sifted with the baking powder. Flatten the dough in the tin and bake for 10–15 minutes until light golden. Remove from the oven and turn the temperature down to 160°C fan (180°C/gas 4).

Mix the filling ingredients together and pour over the pastry base in the tin. Bake for about 5 minutes until just set but still a little wobbly. Remove from the oven and set aside while you make the topping.

Whisk the egg whites to soft peaks, then gradually whisk in the sugar. Spread in peaks over the filling. Bake for 10–15 minutes until crisp and golden. Leave to cool before slicing.

For a sweet, exotic alternative...use the sieved pulp from 12 passionfruit instead of lemon juice in the filling, with half the amount of sugar.

250g plain white flour
2tsp baking powder
200g caster sugar
150ml light olive oil
3 medium organic eggs
Finely grated zest of 2 lemons

FOR THE TOPPING
Finely grated zest of 1 lemon
2tbsp extra virgin olive oil
50g caster sugar

**CUTS INTO
TEN SLICES**

LEMON OLIVE OIL CAKE

Heat the oven to 180°C fan (200°C/gas 6). Grease a 22cm non-stick springform cake tin.

Mix together the grated lemon zest and olive oil for the topping in a small bowl and set aside.

Sift the flour and baking powder into a bowl and stir in the sugar. In a separate bowl, whisk the olive oil with the eggs and lemon zest until combined. Gently fold into the dry ingredients. Spoon the mixture into the cake tin and tap gently to make it level. Bake for 25 minutes until a skewer inserted in the centre comes out clean.

Remove the cake from the oven and prick lots of holes in the top with a skewer. Brush the lemon oil over the cake and sprinkle with the sugar. Return the cake to the oven for 3 minutes to make the sugar glisten. Leave to cool before removing from the tin.

650g granulated sugar

350g limes (about 7 fruit)

LIME MARMALADE

Spread the sugar out on a baking tray and warm in the oven on its lowest setting while you prepare the fruit.

Soften the limes slightly by boiling them in a pan of water for about 3 minutes. Drain and leave until cool enough to handle, then remove the zest with a vegetable peeler and cut into fine shreds. Remove the pith from the limes and tie in a muslin bag. Chop the flesh (discarding any pips or fibrous pieces). Put the flesh, zest, and 850ml cold water in a pan and bring to the boil. Add the muslin bag and boil for 15 minutes.

Lift the muslin bag out of the marmalade and squeeze hard against the inside of the pan to extract all the liquid (this contains pectin, which will help the marmalade set). Discard the bag. Turn the heat down. Add the warm sugar to the marmalade and stir until dissolved. Increase the heat and boil steadily for 15 minutes, stirring from time to time.

To test if the marmalade is ready to come off the heat, place a small spoonful on a chilled saucer, then run the tip of the spoon through the centre – it should separate into two halves. If the marmalade runs back together, continue boiling and retest.

Leave to stand off the heat for 20 minutes, then decant into sterilized Kilner jars and seal while hot. Cool, then keep in the fridge.

For a different flavour...use grapefruit instead of limes.

MANGOES

The best way to tell if a mango is juicy and full of flavour is to pick it up and smell it. Colour is no guide, since perfectly ripe mangoes can be green, yellow, blush-pink, or amber, depending on the variety. The Indian Alfonso is my favourite mango. It's one of the best for perfume and flavour and also for texture, which is as smooth as silk. Some mangoes smell and taste good, but their flesh can be unpleasantly stringy when you bite into it.

1 ripe mango
200g natural yogurt
3tbsp milk
4tbsp clear honey, or more to taste
Leaves picked from 2 sprigs of fresh mint

SERVES TWO   ½tsp ground cardamom or finely crushed cardamom seeds

MANGO LASSI

Peel the mango and remove all of the flesh from the stone. Blitz the flesh to a smooth pulp in a blender. Add the remaining ingredients and blitz again until smooth. Taste for sweetness, adding more honey if you like, then pour into two glasses and serve.

For a more tangy lassi...add a few drops of fresh lime or lemon juice.

2 large ripe mangoes
5 medium organic egg yolks
150g caster sugar
4 leaves gelatine

550ml whipping or double cream

MANGO PARFAIT

Line a 900g loaf tin (23 x 13cm) with cling film.

Peel the mangoes and remove all of the flesh from the stones. Purée the flesh in a blender, then work through a sieve into a pan. Simmer gently over a medium heat until reduced by half. Leave to cool.

Put the egg yolks in a bowl and whisk with an electric mixer on medium speed until the yolks start to turn paler in colour and increase in volume. At the same time, dissolve the sugar in 6tbsp water in a pan, then turn up the heat and boil rapidly for 1 minute. Increase the mixer speed and slowly drizzle the hot sugar syrup down the inside of the bowl on to the yolks. Continue whisking the sabayon until the bowl is cool to the touch. Set aside.

Soak the gelatine in a bowl of cold water for 5 minutes. Meanwhile, bring 50ml of the cream to a gentle simmer in a small pan over a medium heat. Lift the gelatine out of the water and squeeze to remove excess moisture, then drop into the cream, off the heat, and stir well until the gelatine has melted.

Whip the remaining cream to soft peaks, then fold into the mango purée. Pour the liquid cream through a sieve into the mango mixture and stir well, then gently fold in the egg sabayon. Pour the parfait mixture into the loaf tin. Cover and freeze until firm – this will take at least 4 hours. To serve, cut into slices with a warm knife.

12 wonton wrappers, each about 10 x 9cm
Vegetable oil, for brushing
Sea salt and freshly milled black pepper

FOR THE SALSA
1 firm, ripe mango
Finely grated zest and juice of 1 lime
Leaves picked from 3 sprigs of fresh mint, chopped
Leaves picked from 6 sprigs of fresh coriander, chopped
½ shallot, finely diced
½ red pepper, finely diced
A knob of fresh root ginger, peeled and finely grated
Wasabi paste, to taste

**MAKES
TWENTY-FOUR**

MANGO AND
WASABI SALSA
IN WONTON CUPS

Heat the oven to 180°C fan (200°C/gas 6). Oil a 24-hole, non-stick mini muffin tray (or two 12-hole trays).

To make the salsa, peel the mango and remove all the flesh from the stone, then cut the flesh into 5mm dice. Put the mango in a bowl with the lime zest and juice and stir well to mix. Add the remaining salsa ingredients, with wasabi paste, salt, and pepper to taste. Mix well. Cover and chill in the fridge while you make the wonton cups.

Cut the wonton wrappers diagonally in half to make 24 triangles. Press a triangle into each hole in the muffin tray so that two points of the triangle overhang the rim. Brush the wonton triangles with oil and bake for 5 minutes. Lift the wonton cups out of the tray and leave to cool before filling them with the salsa.

Other serving ideas...are to put flaked smoked fish or shredded chicken in the bottom of each cup before filling with salsa. Or use the salsa (without the cups) as a zesty accompaniment for fish or chicken.

PEARS

Only use pears when they're in season, in late summer and autumn. This is when they're ripe, juicy, and sweet, not dry and woolly as they can be at other times of year. Some of the famous varieties you'll see are Conference, Comice, Williams and Bosc. These can all be used in cooking. Also look out for locally grown, less well-known varieties at farm shops and markets, and make the most of these when you find them.

6 ripe Conference or other firm pears
200g granulated sugar
Juice of 2 lemons
25g yellow mustard seeds
MAKES 400ML   25ml white wine vinegar

PEAR AND MUSTARD COMPOTE

Peel and core the pears, then cut into small dice. Place in a pan with all the other ingredients and 50ml cold water. Let the sugar dissolve over a low heat, stirring once or twice, then increase the heat and simmer, stirring regularly, for about an hour. At the end, the compote should have thickened and turned a pale golden colour.

Decant into sterilized Kilner jars and seal while hot. Cool, then keep in the fridge for up to 6 weeks. Serve with cheese or cold meat.

400g caster or granulated sugar
4 star anise
7 ripe Comice pears

FOR THE PASTRY
150g soft unsalted butter
75g icing sugar, sifted
Pinch of fine salt
1 medium organic egg,
    beaten
250g plain white flour

FOR THE FILLING
125g walnut pieces or halves
125g soft unsalted butter
125g caster sugar
3 medium organic eggs, beaten
60g plain white flour

SERVES SIX

PEAR AND WALNUT TART

First make the pastry. Cream the butter and sugar in an electric mixer. Mix in the salt and egg, then mix in the flour until the dough just comes together – don't overwork it. Shape the dough into a square on a floured surface, wrap in cling film, and chill for 30–45 minutes.

Set a 20cm metal ring that is 5–7cm deep on a baking tray lined with non-stick baking parchment. Roll out the pastry until about 4mm thick. Cut out a 30–32cm disc. Line the ring with the pastry, letting it overhang the top. If it cracks, press it together. Chill for at least 30 minutes.

Heat the oven to 180°C fan (200°C/gas 6).

Line the pastry case with non-stick baking parchment and fill to the top with baking beans. Bake for 25 minutes. Remove the paper and beans and bake for 5 minutes. Cool, then trim off the overhanging pastry.

Combine the sugar, star anise, and 1.5 litres water in a large pan. Dissolve the sugar, then bring to the boil. Meanwhile, peel the pears. Cut a circle in the bottom of each fruit and hollow out the core, keeping the outer layer of pear intact. Lower the pears into the poaching liquid, cover with non-stick baking parchment, and poach for 10–15 minutes until tender. Remove the pears and chill in the fridge. Reduce 300ml of the poaching liquid to a syrup.

For the filling, blitz the walnuts to medium-coarse crumbs in a food processor. Cream the butter and sugar, then gradually mix in the eggs and fold in the flour and walnuts. Spread a 2cm layer of filling over the bottom of the tart case. Stand the pears on top in a ring with one in the middle. Spoon the remaining filling around and in between the pears. Bake for 30–40 minutes until the pears and filling are golden. Remove from the oven and brush with the warm syrup. Cool, unmould, and serve.

6 ripe Comice pears
75g caster sugar
3 sprigs of fresh rosemary,
    broken into pieces
50g unsalted butter, diced

TO FINISH
100g block of Parmesan cheese,
    shaved with a vegetable peeler
50g fresh almonds, skinned and
    shredded (optional)
Sea salt

ROSEMARY ROASTED PEARS

Peel the pears and remove the stems, then cut each pear lengthways into quarters. Cut out the cores if you like.

Heat a heavy ovenproof frying pan over a high heat until hot. Put the sugar and rosemary in the pan with a splash of water. Dissolve the sugar over a low to medium heat, then increase the heat and bring to a light caramel, swirling it in the pan from time to time. Do not stir.

Add the butter to the caramel and swirl to combine, then add the pears. Turn down the heat and cook for 10–15 minutes until the pears become dark golden, gently moving and turning them in the caramel.

Meanwhile, heat the oven to 180°C fan (200°C/gas 6).

If necessary, add 50ml cold water to the caramel to smooth it out, then transfer the pan to the oven. Cook for 5 minutes until the pears feel tender when pierced with a skewer.

Serve the pears warm or at room temperature, topped with the Parmesan shavings, almonds (if using), and a sprinkling of sea salt.

These pears are versatile...because they can be served as a starter, or as an accompaniment to roast chicken or pork. Without the Parmesan and salt, they can be served as a dessert with mascarpone or clotted cream.

Fresh almonds are in season...in the summer. Use blanched or toasted almonds at other times of year.

PINEAPPLE

The best pineapples are the small super-sweet varieties that come mostly from Hawaii, Florida, and Costa Rica. They may be expensive, but they are worth it. Preparation is important with any pineapple, no matter what the size, so always dig out each "eye" with the tip of a small, sharp knife. This is time-consuming, but satisfying in the end. If you've got an electric juicer, you can make your own pineapple juice, although the juice in cartons can be very good – as long as it's pure pressed pineapple and not pineapple fruit drink.

1 ripe pineapple
300g caster or granulated sugar
4 star anise
50ml dark rum
SERVES FOUR 6 black peppercorns

PINEAPPLE CARPACCIO

Top and tail the pineapple, then cut off the skin and remove the "eyes". Slice the pineapple crossways into very thin discs. Place these in a shallow rigid container, overlapping them in a single layer.

Put all the remaining ingredients in a pan with 400ml cold water. Dissolve the sugar over a low heat, stirring once or twice, then bring to the boil. Pour the syrup over the pineapple, making sure that every slice is submerged. Cool, then cover and leave to infuse in the fridge overnight. Drain off the liquid before serving, as an accompaniment for chicken, pork, or fish, or as a refreshing dessert with ice cream.

½ ripe pineapple
150g mascarpone
50g icing sugar, sifted
Seeds scraped from ¼ vanilla pod
1 heaped tbsp finely sliced fresh mint

50g meringues (nests or shells), lightly crushed

PINEAPPLE TIANS WITH MASCARPONE AND MINT

Top and tail the pineapple, then cut off the skin and remove the "eyes". Cut the flesh into 5mm dice, discarding the core. Place the pineapple dice on kitchen paper to absorb excess moisture – the pineapple needs to be really dry.

Just before serving, beat the mascarpone with the icing sugar and vanilla seeds in a bowl until just thickened. Fold in the mint and almost all of the diced pineapple and crushed meringues.

To make each tian, stand a metal ring, about 5cm in diameter and 7.5cm tall, on a serving plate. Fill with one-quarter of the pineapple mixture, pressing it down well. Lift off the ring and top the tian with one-quarter of the remaining meringue. Repeat to make three more tians. Decorate the edges of the plates with the remaining diced pineapple and serve immediately.

100g caster sugar
1 litre pineapple juice
100ml Malibu

PINEAPPLE
AND MALIBU
GRANITA

Put the sugar in a pan with 100ml cold water. Heat gently until the sugar has dissolved, stirring once or twice, then bring to the boil. Add the pineapple juice and Malibu and stir well to mix.

Cool, then freeze in a large plastic tray until frozen. This should take about 4 hours. Whisk the granita well after the first hour to prevent large ice crystals from forming. When fully frozen, scrape with a fork to make a slushy texture. Keep in a rigid container in the freezer for up to 1 week.

RHUBARB

There are two types of rhubarb. Early forced rhubarb grown indoors is in season in January and February. Its flavour is exceptionally sweet, and its delicate candy-pink stems only need trimming before use. Outdoor-grown rhubarb has a short season in early summer, and you need to catch it quick before it turns woody. Only use this type of rhubarb when it's young, and peel off any tough strings first or it will be tough.

750g young or forced rhubarb
200g caster sugar, or more to taste

FOR THE CRUMBLE
80g unsalted butter, diced
100g plain white flour
50g Demerara sugar
SERVES SIX   80g rolled oats

RHUBARB CRUMBLES

Heat the oven to 180°C fan (200°C/gas 6).

Trim the rhubarb and peel if necessary, then cut into 2cm-long pieces. Place in a pan with the sugar. Cook over a low heat, stirring occasionally, until the sugar has dissolved and the rhubarb juices are beginning to run. Increase the heat to medium and continue cooking until the rhubarb is tender and juicy. This should take 6–10 minutes, depending on the age and thickness of the rhubarb. Taste for sweetness. Divide among six individual ovenproof dishes and set them on a baking tray.

To make the crumble topping, rub the butter into the flour until the mixture looks like breadcrumbs, then stir in the sugar and oats. Sprinkle evenly over the rhubarb. Bake for about 20 minutes until golden.

For a large crumble...use a 1.5-litre baking dish (approx 17 x 20 x 5cm) and bake for about 40 minutes.

Instead of rhubarb...use gooseberries or halved plums.

500g young or forced rhubarb
250g caster sugar
5 medium organic egg yolks
Rosewater, to taste

250ml whipping or double cream

RHUBARB AND
ROSEWATER PARFAIT

Place eight 250ml glasses in the freezer.

Trim the rhubarb and peel if necessary, then chop into small pieces. Place in a pan with 100g of the sugar and cook over a low heat, stirring occasionally, until the sugar has dissolved and the rhubarb juices are beginning to run. Increase the heat to medium and continue cooking for about 20 minutes until the rhubarb is soft. Cool, then blitz to a purée with a hand blender.

Put the egg yolks in the bowl of your electric mixer and whisk on medium speed until paler in colour, thickened, and fluffy. Meanwhile, dissolve the remaining sugar in 5tbsp water with a few drops of rosewater in a pan over a low heat. Bring to the boil and boil rapidly for 4 minutes. Pour the sugar syrup slowly on to the egg yolks with the machine running on high speed, and continue whisking until the bowl no longer feels warm to the touch and the sabayon is pale and thick. Taste and add more rosewater to get the flavour you like.

Whip the cream to soft peaks, then fold into the rhubarb purée followed by the cold sabayon. Pour into the frozen glasses and return to the freezer. Freeze for 1–2 hours before serving.

400g young or forced rhubarb
100g clear honey, or more to taste
100g mascarpone
200ml double or whipping cream

FOR THE TOPPING
50g caster sugar
2 sticks of young or forced rhubarb,
    peeled and sliced
A splash of grenadine (optional)

RHUBARB FOOL
WITH POACHED
RHUBARB

Trim the rhubarb and peel if necessary, then chop into small chunks. Place in a pan with the honey. Cook over a low heat for 20 minutes until reduced to a soft pulp, stirring occasionally. Leave to cool.

To make the topping, put the sugar in a pan with 100ml cold water and heat gently until the sugar has dissolved, stirring once or twice, then bring to the boil. Add the rhubarb, lower the heat, and poach gently for 6–10 minutes until tender. Remove from the heat and stir in the grenadine, if using, then cool and refrigerate.

Stir the mascarpone in a bowl until smooth, then beat in the honeyed rhubarb pulp. Whip the cream to soft peaks and fold into the rhubarb and mascarpone mix until evenly combined. Taste for sweetness and add more honey if you like. Divide among four glass dishes, cover, and refrigerate for at least an hour.

Serve the fools topped with the poached rhubarb.

For a change...use blueberries instead of rhubarb. Cook them for 6–10 minutes to make the fool, and poach them for 3–5 minutes for the topping.

STONE FRUIT

Apricots, nectarines, and peaches have a very short summer season, and when they are perfectly ripe their intense perfume and sweetness are just incomparable. There really is no point in buying them at other times of year. Plums come later, and last longer, so there's more opportunity to use them, in savoury as well as sweet dishes. They add freshness to rich meats like duck, offal, and game, in the same way that lemons do with fish.

125ml dark rum
100g soft brown sugar
Finely grated zest and juice of 2 limes
8 ripe peaches

SERVES SIX Leaves picked from 1 large bunch of fresh mint, chopped

PEACHES WITH RUM AND MINT

Warm the rum and sugar in a small pan over a low heat until the sugar has dissolved. Bring to the boil, then remove from the heat and swirl in the lime zest and juice.

Halve and stone the peaches, and cut into chunky dice. Put them in a bowl with the mint, pour in the warm syrup, and stir gently to mix. Cover and refrigerate for a couple of hours before serving.

Instead of peaches...use ripe nectarines or double the amount of apricots.

100g caster sugar
8 ripe red-skinned plums, quartered and stoned
1 cinnamon stick
1 star anise
1tsp ground mixed spice
100ml port
Olive oil
2 pieces of fresh foie gras, each weighing 60–80g

SERVES FOUR   Sea salt and freshly milled black pepper

SPICED PLUMS
WITH SAUTÉED
FOIE GRAS

Heat a heavy frying pan over a high heat until hot. Add the sugar and gently shake the pan so that the sugar spreads evenly and melts to form a very light golden caramel – this should take 3–5 minutes. Add the plums and all the spices, and shake the pan gently to coat the plums in the caramel. When the plums are lightly coloured, swirl in the port and turn the heat right down. Cook for about 10 minutes until soft and syrupy, swirling the contents of the pan frequently.

For the foie gras, heat a little olive oil in a frying pan over a medium to high heat until hot. Season the foie gras, then place in the pan and sauté for 2 minutes on each side until nicely coloured, basting constantly with the hot oil. Remove from the pan and leave to rest for 2 minutes before serving with the plums.

For an attractive presentation...before cooking, score the sides of the foie gras in a diamond pattern with the back of a knife blade.

30g caster sugar
20ml olive oil
20ml brandy
8 ripe apricots, halved and stoned

FOR THE AMARETTI CREAM
100ml double or whipping cream
100g natural Greek yogurt
50g amaretti, crushed

CARAMELIZED APRICOTS WITH AMARETTI CREAM

First make the amaretti cream. Whip the cream to soft peaks in a bowl, then fold in the yogurt and crushed amaretti. Cover and refrigerate.

Heat a heavy frying pan over a high heat until hot. Add the sugar and gently shake the pan so that the sugar spreads evenly, then leave without stirring over a low to medium heat until the sugar melts and forms a very light golden caramel. This should take 5–8 minutes, depending on the heat and pan used. Carefully add the olive oil and brandy (it may splutter), and then the apricots, skin-side up. Swirl gently to combine.

Cook until the apricots have coloured slightly. Turn them over and reduce the heat to low, then continue cooking until the apricots are soft. The total cooking time should be about 4 minutes.

Serve the apricots warm or cold, with the chilled amaretti cream.

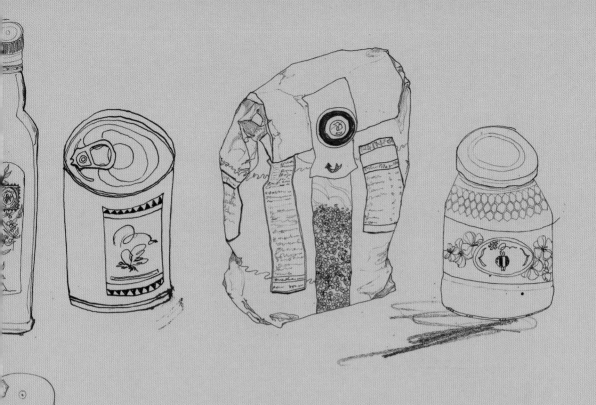

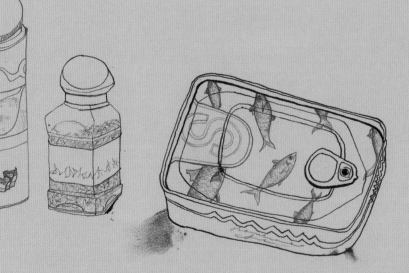

STORECUPBOARD

DARK CHOCOLATE

"If a wine isn't good enough to drink, it shouldn't be used for cooking."
The same is true of chocolate – if you don't enjoy eating it straight from
the wrapper, then don't use it to cook with. Good-quality dark chocolate
has a cocoa solids content of at least 60 per cent, so check the label
before you buy and don't settle for anything less.

80g dark chocolate
100g shelled pistachios
250g plain white flour
125g caster sugar
3 large organic eggs

MAKES TWENTY Finely grated zest of 1 orange

CHOCOLATE
AND PISTACHIO
BISCOTTI

Heat the oven to 170°C fan (190°C/gas 5). Grease a large baking tray.

Chop the chocolate and pistachios into chunky pieces, then combine
in a bowl with the flour and sugar. Beat the eggs with the orange zest in
another bowl. Add three-quarters of the eggs to the dry ingredients and
stir well with a wooden spoon. Gradually stir in enough of the remaining
egg mixture until you have a dough that is quite stiff, but not crumbly.

Tip the dough on to a floured surface and with floured hands shape
into a 20 x 4cm log. Place the log on the tray and bake for 20 minutes.
Transfer to a rack and leave to cool to room temperature. Turn the oven
up to 180°C fan (200°C/gas 6), and grease the tray again.

Place the log on a board and cut into twenty 1cm-thick slices. Lay the
slices on the tray (or on two trays if they won't all fit on one). Bake for
6 minutes. Turn the biscotti over and bake for another 6 minutes. Cool
on a rack, then store in an airtight container to retain the crunch.

For a change...use toasted hazelnuts or chopped dried
apricots instead of pistachios.

200g dark chocolate
300ml milk
300ml whipping or double cream
6 medium organic egg yolks
160g caster sugar
3 medium organic egg whites

SERVES SIX

Grated dark chocolate, to serve

CHOCOLATE ICE CREAM

Break the chocolate into pieces and place in a large bowl; set aside.
Bring the milk and 100ml of the cream to the boil in a pan. Whisk the
egg yolks with 80g of the sugar in another bowl until smooth, then whisk
in a little of the hot cream. Pour this mixture into the pan of cream and
mix thoroughly with a rubber spatula. Stir constantly over a low heat
until the custard is thick enough to coat the back of the spatula.

Strain the custard through a fine sieve on to the chocolate. Leave for
5 minutes, then whisk well until smooth. Transfer to a shallow container
and cover the surface of the custard with cling film to prevent a skin
from forming. Chill in the fridge until cold.

Whip the remaining 200ml cream to soft peaks and fold into the
cold chocolate custard. Whisk the egg whites to soft peaks, then slowly
whisk in the remaining 80g sugar to make a meringue. Add one-quarter
of the meringue to the custard cream and mix together well. Fold in the
remaining meringue until evenly combined.

Transfer the mixture to a freezer container and cover with cling film
and the lid. Freeze until firm – this should take 2–4 hours. There's no
need to churn in an ice-cream maker as the whipped cream and egg
whites make this ice cream beautifully smooth. The ice cream can
be kept in the freezer for up to 3 days.

Serve in scoops, topped with grated chocolate.

100g dark chocolate, broken into pieces
100g unsalted butter, diced
3 medium organic eggs, separated
125g ground almonds

100g caster sugar
100g dark chocolate chips

GOOEY CHOCOLATE SLICE

Heat the oven to 160°C fan (180°C/gas 4). Grease a 20 x 15 x 7.5cm baking tin and line with non-stick baking parchment.

Melt the chocolate and butter in a bowl set over a pan of gently simmering water. Remove the bowl from the pan and whisk in the egg yolks followed by the almonds.

Whisk the egg whites to stiff peaks, then slowly whisk in the sugar to make a meringue. Gently fold one-quarter of the meringue into the chocolate mixture and mix until smooth. Add the rest of the meringue and the chocolate chips, and fold together until evenly combined.

Transfer the mixture to the tin and bake for 20 minutes. Leave to settle for 15–30 minutes, then lift out on the paper and slice. Serve warm with crème fraîche for a dessert, or cold as a cake with tea or coffee.

COUSCOUS

Made from grains of semolina (coarsely ground durum wheat), couscous is a great ingredient to keep in the storecupboard: it's quick and easy to prepare, needs no cooking, and can be served as a main dish or side, either hot or cold. For a change, try giant Israeli couscous, which you can find in ethnic shops and markets.

1 butternut squash, weighing about 750g,
  peeled, deseeded, and diced into chunks
200g couscous
½tsp fine salt
400ml boiling water, or chicken or vegetable stock
A little light olive oil or vegetable oil
100g pumpkin seeds
2tbsp toasted sesame oil
Leaves picked from 1 small bunch of fresh coriander,
  roughly chopped
Sea salt and freshly milled black pepper

SERVES FOUR

ROAST SQUASH AND CORIANDER COUSCOUS

Heat the oven to 180°C fan (200°C/gas 6). Oil a large baking tray.
Spread the squash out in a single layer on the tray and season. Roast for 20–30 minutes until tender and nicely coloured.

Meanwhile, put the couscous and fine salt in a large bowl. Pour over the boiling water or stock and mix well. Cover the bowl tightly with cling film and set aside in a warm place to soak for about 15 minutes.

Heat a little olive oil in a small frying pan over a medium heat. Add the pumpkin seeds, season, and fry for a few minutes until they begin to swell and look toasted.

Take the cling film off the bowl of couscous. Fork through the couscous to separate the grains, then fork through the sesame oil. Fold in the pumpkin seeds, squash, and coriander, and taste for seasoning.

In the autumn and winter months...you can use pumpkin instead of butternut squash.

200g couscous
½tsp fine salt
400ml boiling water, or chicken or vegetable stock
2tsp cumin seeds
1tsp ground cinnamon
1tsp turmeric
½tsp chilli powder
3tbsp olive oil
1 onion, halved and sliced
200g drained canned or cooked chickpeas
¼ fresh pineapple, peeled, cored, and cut into chunks
50g pine nuts, toasted

SERVES FOUR   Sea salt and freshly milled black pepper

COUSCOUS WITH
SPICED CHICKPEAS
AND PINEAPPLE

Put the couscous and fine salt in a large bowl, pour over the boiling water or stock, and mix well. Cover the bowl tightly with cling film and leave in a warm place to soak for about 15 minutes.

Meanwhile, heat a griddle pan over a medium to high heat until hot. At the same time, scatter the spices in a dry frying pan and toast over a medium heat for a few minutes until fragrant. Add 2tbsp of the oil and the onion slices to the spices and sauté for a few minutes until the onion is soft. Add the chickpeas and toss until heated through. Remove from the heat and keep warm.

Coat the pineapple in the remaining oil and place on the hot griddle pan. Cook for a few minutes until charred on all sides.

Take the cling film off the bowl of couscous. Fork through the couscous to separate the grains, then fork through the spiced chickpeas, pineapple, and pine nuts. Season to taste before serving.

Light olive oil or vegetable oil
4 shallots, finely sliced into rings
Leaves picked from 1 small bunch of fresh thyme,
    roughly chopped
25g caster or granulated sugar
5tbsp balsamic vinegar
200g couscous
½tsp fine salt
400ml boiling water, or chicken or vegetable stock
25g unsalted butter
100g walnut halves or pieces
2tbsp walnut oil or olive oil
Sea salt and freshly milled black pepper

A few small sprigs of fresh thyme, to finish

WALNUT AND CARAMELIZED SHALLOT COUSCOUS

Heat a little olive oil in a frying pan. Add the shallots, thyme, and some seasoning, and sauté over a medium heat for a few minutes until the shallots are soft and golden. Add the sugar followed by the vinegar and mix well. Leave to caramelize over a low heat, stirring occasionally, while you continue with the rest of the recipe.

Put the couscous and fine salt in a large bowl, pour over the boiling water or stock, and mix well. Cover the bowl tightly with cling film and set aside in a warm place to soak for about 15 minutes.

Heat the butter in a frying pan over a medium heat until it begins to foam. Add the walnuts and a good pinch of sea salt, and cook for a few minutes until the nuts are golden, moving them around in the pan to prevent them from burning. Tip the nuts on to kitchen paper and leave to drain.

When the shallots are caramelized and all the liquid has evaporated, remove the pan from the heat. Take the cling film off the bowl of couscous and fork through the couscous to separate the grains. Fork through the shallots, walnuts, walnut oil, and thyme sprigs. Taste for seasoning before serving.

If you prefer...use pecans instead of walnuts.

FLOUR

It seems there's a different flour for just about everything. Plain flour is the one for every day: for thickening and coating, for making sauces and pancakes, pastry and cookies, and some cakes. Strong flour is essential for bread because it contains a high amount of gluten, which helps dough rise. And if you make your own pasta, you'll know you need Italian "oo", a fine flour that makes kneading and rolling easy, and gives a silky-smooth result.

125g soft unsalted butter
200g caster sugar
4tsp finely grated orange zest
    (from 2 oranges)
3 medium organic eggs,
    beaten

TO FINISH

150g plain white flour
1tsp baking powder
4tbsp crème fraîche

125g caster sugar
4tbsp fresh orange juice
Finely shredded zest of 1 orange

**MAKES TWENTY
TO TWENTY-TWO**

ORANGE
SYRUP CAKES

Heat the oven to 160°C fan (180°C/gas 4). Grease two mini muffin trays (each with 10 or 11 holes).

Cream the butter with the sugar and orange zest. Add the eggs and mix well. Sift in the flour and baking powder, and mix until almost combined. Fold in the crème fraîche. Spoon the mixture into the muffin trays. Bake for 15–20 minutes until a toothpick inserted in the centre of a cake comes out clean. Remove the trays from the oven.

To finish, dissolve 25g of the sugar in the orange juice, then bring to the boil. Drizzle this syrup over the cakes while they are still hot.

Put the orange zest in a small pan of water and bring to the boil, then drain and refresh under the cold tap. Repeat this blanching procedure twice. Return the zest to the pan and add the remaining sugar and 50ml water. Heat gently until the sugar has dissolved, then boil for 5 minutes until the zest is thickly coated in syrup.

Turn the cakes out of the trays and spoon over the syrupy zest. Serve warm with custard for a dessert, or cold just as they are with tea or coffee.

350g plain white flour
2tbsp ground mixed spice
1tsp fine salt
15g caster sugar
1tsp fast-action dried yeast
3 medium organic eggs, beaten
6tbsp milk
75g soft unsalted butter

TO FINISH
1 medium organic egg yolk, lightly beaten

CUTS INTO
TWELVE SLICES

1tbsp sea salt
2tbsp ground mixed spice

SPICED BRIOCHE

Sift the flour and mixed spice into the bowl of your electric mixer. Dot the flour with the salt, sugar, and yeast, and put the eggs and milk in the middle. Mix on low speed to make a smooth dough. Increase the speed to high and work until the dough comes away from the side of the bowl. With the machine running, slowly work in the butter until evenly incorporated. Cover the bowl and leave the dough to rise in the fridge overnight – it will about double its original size.

Heat the oven to 200°C fan (220°C/gas 7). Grease a 500g brioche tin or loaf tin.

Turn the dough on to a floured surface and knead for 2 minutes, then shape into a loaf and place in the tin. Brush the top with the egg yolk and sprinkle with the sea salt and spice. Bake for 20 minutes. To test if the brioche is cooked, tip it out of the tin and tap the base with your knuckles: it should sound hollow.

Slow rising in the fridge...develops the flavours of the butter and yeast in the dough, but if you're in a hurry you can rise the dough in a warm place – it should take 1–2 hours to almost double in size.

300g strong white bread flour
175g polenta
1½tsp fast-action dried yeast
1tsp fine salt
2tsp caster sugar
½tsp smoked paprika
2½tbsp cumin seeds, toasted and lightly crushed
50ml vegetable oil
225ml lukewarm water
330g can sweetcorn kernels, drained and patted
    dry on kitchen paper
25g fresh dill, roughly chopped

CUTS INTO
TWENTY SLICES 20g unsalted butter, melted
Sea salt and cracked black pepper

CUMIN CORNBREAD

Place the flour, polenta, yeast, fine salt, sugar, paprika, and cumin in the bowl of your electric mixer fitted with the dough hook attachment, and mix slowly together. Mix the oil and water in a jug. Slowly add to the dry ingredients, mixing until they come together, adding another tablespoon of warm water if necessary. Add the sweetcorn. Increase the speed and mix for 5 minutes to knead the dough.

Transfer the dough to an oiled large bowl and cover with cling film. Leave to rise in a warm place for 45 minutes to 1 hour until the dough is about double its original size.

Turn the dough on to a floured surface and knock back. Knead in the chopped dill. Knead for a further 5 minutes, then shape into a rectangular loaf (about 28 x 17cm) on a floured baking tray. Dust with flour and cover loosely with cling film. Leave the loaf in a warm place for 10–20 minutes until it rises half as much again.

Meanwhile, heat the oven to 190°C fan (210°C/gas 6½).

Bake the bread for 20 minutes. Remove and brush with the melted butter, then sprinkle with sea salt and black pepper. Bake for a further 5–10 minutes until golden. Cool on a rack before serving.

To make the dough by hand...follow the instructions above, kneading on a floured surface for 5 minutes.

GOLDEN SYRUP

Traditional recipes like gingerbread, sticky toffee pudding, and treacle tart wouldn't taste the same without golden syrup – it's so much more than a sweetener. Its depth of flavour and intense sweetness are totally unique, and impossible to describe. An added advantage is that when you heat it up, it doesn't crystallize like sugar syrup and caramel tend to do.

200g golden syrup
150g soft unsalted butter
75g caster sugar
1 medium organic egg, beaten
250g plain white flour
2tbsp ground ginger
1½tsp ground cinnamon
½tsp fine salt

CUTS INTO 100ml milk
FOURTEEN 1tsp bicarbonate of soda
SLICES Demerara sugar, to finish

GINGERBREAD

Heat the oven to 160°C fan (180°C/gas 4). Thoroughly grease a 19 x 12cm loaf tin that is 8cm deep (about 1-litre capacity). Line the bottom with non-stick baking parchment.

Gently heat the golden syrup in a pan until just slightly runny. Cream the butter with the sugar, then beat in the syrup and egg. Sift the flour with the spices and fine salt, and fold into the creamed mixture. Warm the milk and dissolve the bicarbonate of soda in it, then fold into the creamed mixture (it is quite runny).

Pour the mixture into the tin and sprinkle with Demerara sugar. Bake for about 1 hour until a skewer inserted in the centre comes out clean. If the gingerbread is browning too much towards the end of the baking time, cover it with foil. Leave to cool in the tin for about 20 minutes, then remove and cool on a rack before slicing.

150g ready-to-eat soft dried dates, chopped
75g soft unsalted butter
175g golden syrup
2 medium organic eggs, beaten
50ml milk
1tsp bicarbonate of soda
125g plain white flour
Pinch of fine salt

FOR THE SAUCE
4tbsp golden syrup
¼tsp fine salt
125ml whipping or double cream

MAKES SIX

STICKY TOFFEE PUDDINGS

Heat the oven to 180°C fan (200°C/gas 6). Grease six 200ml pudding moulds and set them on a baking tray.

Simmer the chopped dates with 175ml water in a small pan, stirring regularly, until they soften to a chunky purée. Cream the butter with 100g of the golden syrup until creamy, then mix in the eggs. Heat the milk in a pan until almost boiling. Stir in the bicarbonate of soda, then beat into the creamed mixture. Stir in the dates, then fold in the flour and fine salt to give a fairly runny mix.

Heat the remaining 75g golden syrup with 50ml water in a pan. Pour into the moulds, then spoon in the pudding mixture. Bake for 15 minutes until a skewer inserted into a pudding comes out clean.

For the sauce, put the golden syrup and salt in a pan and bring to a gentle simmer. Slowly whisk in the cream and simmer for 5 minutes.

Turn the puddings out, drizzle over the sauce, and serve hot, with ice cream or crème fraîche.

To make a large pudding...use a 1-litre bowl set on a baking tray and bake for 30 minutes.

100g golden syrup
150g Demerara sugar
75g unsalted butter, cut in pieces
3tbsp clear honey
3tbsp dark rum
Pinch of fine salt
3 medium organic eggs, beaten
150g pecan halves, roughly chopped

FOR THE PASTRY
150g soft unsalted butter
75g icing sugar, sifted
¼tsp fine salt
1 medium organic egg, beaten
250g plain white flour

MAKES EIGHT

PECAN TARTS

First make the pastry. Beat the butter with the sugar in an electric mixer, using the paddle attachment. Add the salt and egg and mix well, then sift in the flour in two batches and mix until the dough just comes together. Don't overwork it. Turn on to a floured surface and shape into a square. Wrap in cling film and firm up in the fridge for 30 minutes to 1 hour.

Take eight 9–10cm metal rings that are 2cm deep and stand them on one or two baking trays lined with non-stick baking parchment. Divide the dough in half and roll out each piece on a floured surface until about 4mm thick. Cut out a total of eight 12cm discs using a plain cutter, or the rim of a cup or saucer. Line the rings with the dough, easing it in and making sure it fits neatly into the bottom edges. Trim the tops flush, if necessary. Leave to rest in the fridge for 15 minutes.

Heat the oven to 180°C fan (200°C/gas 6).

For the filling, gently heat the golden syrup in a pan with the sugar, butter, honey, rum, and salt until the sugar has dissolved. Allow to cool a little, then whisk in the eggs and nuts. Set aside.

Line the pastry cases with non-stick baking parchment and fill with baking beans or rice. Bake blind for 10 minutes. Remove from the oven and carefully lift out the paper and beans. Return the pastry cases to the oven to bake for a further 5 minutes.

Turn the oven down to 160°C fan (180°C/gas 4). Spoon the filling into the pastry cases and bake for 12–15 minutes until set.

Instead of metal rings...use loose-bottomed tartlet tins.

To make a large tart...shape the pastry dough into a round instead of a square before chilling. Use a 23cm metal ring or loose-bottomed tart tin and bake blind for 15 minutes plus 10 minutes, then for 25–30 minutes with the filling.

LENTILS

Red, green, and Puy – these are the three most useful lentils to keep in the storecupboard. All pulses need soaking before cooking, and lentils are no exception – whatever the packet or recipe says. Soaking softens lentils, which makes them cook more quickly and evenly. Seasoning should always be left to the very end, because salt in the cooking water will toughen the skins and prevent the lentils from becoming tender.

150g green lentils, soaked in cold water
    for at least 4 hours
1 carrot, peeled and halved crossways
1 leek (white and green parts), trimmed
    and halved crossways
2 bay leaves
1 small bunch of fresh thyme, tied with string
About 500ml hot chicken or vegetable stock
100ml double or whipping cream

SERVES FOUR Sea salt and freshly milled black pepper

LENTIL VELOUTÉ

Drain and rinse the lentils, then place in a large pan with the carrot, leek, and herbs. Cover well with cold water and bring to the boil. Simmer for about 20 minutes until the lentils are tender.

Drain the lentils, and discard the vegetables and herbs. Put the lentils in a blender and add 250ml of the stock. Blitz until smooth. Pass the purée through a fine sieve into a clean pan and whisk in another 250ml stock and the cream. Season to taste. Reheat before serving, adjusting the consistency with more stock or water, if necessary.

250g red lentils, soaked in cold water
for at least 4 hours
1tbsp cumin seeds
1tbsp turmeric
1tsp black mustard seeds
½tsp chilli powder
Vegetable oil
1 onion, finely sliced
3 garlic cloves, crushed
200ml sieved canned tomatoes
1tsp Demerara sugar
½tsp fine salt
Sea salt and freshly milled black pepper

SERVES FOUR

FOR THE NAAN
250g plain white flour
1tsp fine salt
1tsp fast-action dried yeast
175ml lukewarm water
1tbsp toasted sesame oil
20g sesame seeds, toasted
Light olive oil

DHAL WITH
SESAME NAAN

To make the naan dough, combine the flour, fine salt, and yeast in your electric mixer, using the dough hook on slow speed. Mix the water and oil together. Slowly add to the dry ingredients with the machine running, then mix for 5 minutes to knead the dough. Transfer to an oiled large bowl and cover with cling film. Leave in a warm place to rise until the dough is double its original size. This should take 30 minutes to 1 hour.

Drain and rinse the lentils, then place in a large pan and cover well with cold water. Bring to the boil and simmer for 6 minutes. Toast the spices in a dry pan for a few minutes until fragrant. Add a little oil, the onion, and garlic, and sauté until the onion is tender.

Drain the lentils and mix into the onion with the tomatoes, sugar, fine salt, and pepper. Simmer gently for 20–30 minutes, stirring occasionally, until thick. Add a splash of water if the dhal gets too dry.

Turn the risen dough on to a floured surface and knead in 15g of the sesame seeds. Divide into 12–15 balls and roll out each into a 12cm disc.

Heat a touch of olive oil in a non-stick frying pan until very hot. Cook the naan, in batches, for 1–2 minutes until puffed up and tinged golden brown underneath. Turn the bread over, splash with a little more oil, and cook the other side for the same amount of time.

Taste the dhal for seasoning, then turn into a serving dish and grind a little sea salt over the top. Sprinkle the naan with olive oil, sea salt, and the remaining sesame seeds.

150g Puy lentils, soaked in cold water
for at least 4 hours
500g Jersey Royal potatoes
4tbsp olive oil
A few sprigs of fresh thyme
15g unsalted butter
20g fresh chervil or flat-leaf parsley
leaves, chopped
Sea salt and freshly milled black pepper

Crème fraîche, to serve

PUY LENTILS
WITH CRUSHED
POTATOES AND
CRÈME FRAÎCHE

Drain and rinse the lentils, then place in a large pan and cover well with cold water. Bring to the boil. Simmer steadily over a medium heat for 20–30 minutes until the lentils are tender, then drain.

Put the potatoes in a pan of salted cold water and bring to the boil. Lower the heat, cover, and simmer for 15–20 minutes until tender when pierced with a knife. Drain and leave until cool enough to handle, then peel off the skins with a small, sharp knife. Place the potatoes in a large bowl and crush into pieces with a fork. Keep the potatoes warm.

Pour the olive oil into a frying pan, place over a medium heat, and add the lentils, thyme, butter, and seasoning. Cook, stirring, until the lentils begin to pop. Add to the potatoes together with the chervil and seasoning. Fold together gently. Serve warm, topped with crème fraîche.

DRIED FRUIT AND NUTS

You get what you pay for with dried fruit, so I always buy the best brands to be sure of plumpness and flavour. Look out for semi-dried or *mi-cuit* fruits that are exceptionally soft and juicy. If you keep dried fruits for a long time they can go hard, but you can remedy this easily by soaking them in brandy, rum, kirsch, or vodka to plump them up. When using nuts in cooking, it's important they're fresh. They go stale very quickly, so keep them in airtight containers and use within a month.

250g rye flour
100g plain wholemeal flour
60g walnut pieces, toasted
2½tsp fast-action dried yeast
1tsp fine salt
2tbsp golden syrup

CUTS INTO   20ml olive oil
TWELVE SLICES   200ml warm water

WALNUT AND RYE BREAD

Place the flours, nuts, yeast, and salt in the bowl of your electric mixer, and mix slowly together using the dough hook attachment. Mix the golden syrup, oil, and water in a jug. Slowly add to the dry ingredients, mixing until they come together. Increase the mixer speed and mix for 5 minutes until a dough is formed. Transfer the dough to an oiled large bowl and cover with cling film. Leave to rise in a warm place for about 45 minutes until the dough puffs up slightly.

Turn the dough on to a floured surface and knock back, then knead it for 5 minutes. Form into a rough rectangular loaf shape on a greased baking tray. Cover loosely with cling film and leave to rest in a warm place for 10–15 minutes while you heat the oven to 180°C fan (200°C/gas 6).

Bake the bread for 20 minutes until golden. Remove and cool on a rack before cutting into 1cm-thick slices.

125g unsalted butter, diced
190g caster sugar
5–6 large organic egg whites
125g ground almonds
25g plain white flour

ALMOND
BUTTER CAKES

Melt the butter in a pan over a medium heat. When it bubbles, whisk with a balloon whisk over the heat until it turns a light brown colour. This should take 5–7 minutes. Remove from the heat, pour into a heatproof jug, and set aside.

Put the remaining ingredients in a bowl and beat with an electric mixer or wooden spoon until the mixture just comes together. Slowly trickle in the butter, mixing well after each addition, until it has all been absorbed. Cover the bowl and chill in the fridge for about an hour.

Heat the oven to 180°C fan (200°C/gas 6). Lightly grease three mini muffin trays, each with 10–12 holes. If you only have one muffin tray, bake the cakes in three batches.

Fill the moulds with the mixture. Bake for 9 minutes until golden. Cool, either in the moulds or on a rack, before serving with afternoon tea, or as petits fours with coffee.

These little cakes...are called *financiers* in French. At the restaurant we make them in 4 x 1.5cm financier moulds, which you can get from specialist kitchen shops. For a neat, professional finish, we pipe the mixture into the moulds.

75g golden raisins
75g currants
50g chopped mixed peel
75g unsalted butter, diced
75g Demerara sugar
Finely grated zest of 1 orange
1tsp ground cinnamon
½tsp freshly grated nutmeg

FOR THE PASTRY
250g chilled unsalted butter
250g plain white flour
1½tsp fine salt
125ml iced water
Milk and granulated sugar, for glazing

ECCLES CAKES

First make the pastry. Remove the butter from the fridge 10 minutes before you want to use it. Sift the flour and salt into a bowl and partially rub in the butter, leaving small lumps. Bind together with the iced water. Shape into a rough rectangle on a floured surface, wrap in cling film, and leave to rest in the fridge for 30 minutes.

Roll out the pastry on a floured surface into a rectangle measuring about 30 x 20cm. Fold in the short edges just to meet in the centre, then fold in half lengthways. Wrap in cling film and refrigerate for 30 minutes Repeat the rolling out, folding, and chilling procedure two more times. Finally, roll out the pastry to 5mm thickness (if more manageable, cut the pastry in half before rolling out). Place on a cling-filmed baking tray, cover with more cling film, and leave to rest in the fridge for 30 minutes.

Meanwhile, make the filling. Combine the fruit and peel in a bowl. Gently melt the butter in a pan with the sugar, orange zest, and spices. Add to the fruit and mix well. Set aside to cool.

Cut out fifteen to twenty 9cm discs from the pastry, stacking them between non-stick baking parchment.

To assemble, lay the pastry discs on a floured surface and place a teaspoonful of filling in the centre of each one. Fold the edges of each disc into the centre, over the filling, and press to seal. Flip the cakes over and carefully press down with the palm of your hand to flatten slightly. Make three small, parallel incisions in the top of each cake, then place them on a tray and keep in the fridge or freezer until ready to bake.

Heat the oven to 200°C fan (220°C/gas 7). Line a baking tray with non-stick baking parchment.

Place the cakes on the parchment, brush with milk, and sprinkle liberally with sugar. Bake for 12–15 minutes until golden. Serve warm or at room temperature.

If baking from frozen...the cakes will need about 15 minutes.

PASTA

Only buy good-quality Italian pasta, preferably made with egg (*all'uovo*), and boil it in lots of salted water. Pasta needs salt while it's cooking or it won't have flavour – once it's cooked it's too late to add salt because it won't absorb it in the same way. Never rely on a timer to tell you that pasta is done. The only way to be sure is to scoop out a piece and try it. Perfectly cooked pasta should be *al dente* – tender but with a slight bite.

100g rocket
100g cashew nuts, toasted
40g Parmesan cheese, freshly grated
100ml extra virgin olive oil, plus a little extra
500g dried linguine

SERVES FOUR Sea salt and freshly milled black pepper

LINGUINE WITH ROCKET AND CASHEW PESTO

Blitz the rocket, nuts, cheese, and 50ml of the oil in a blender until the consistency is like pesto. Add the remaining 50ml oil and blitz again until combined. Season to taste.

Coil the linguine into a large pan of boiling salted water. Boil for 10–12 minutes, or according to packet instructions, until *al dente*. Drain and return to the pan.

Toss the linguine with a little olive oil to prevent sticking, then add the pesto and toss to coat all the pasta strands. Serve immediately, drizzled with extra olive oil and sprinkled with sea salt.

400g dried penne or other short pasta shapes
100g sunblush tomatoes in oil, chopped
100g watercress, large stalks removed
100g blue Stilton cheese
Sea salt and freshly milled black pepper

PENNE WITH SUNBLUSH TOMATOES AND WATERCRESS

Plunge the pasta into a large pan of boiling salted water. Boil for 10–12 minutes, or according to packet instructions, until *al dente*. Drain and return to the pan. Stir through the tomatoes and their oil, then add the watercress and seasoning to taste and mix well. Serve immediately, with the cheese crumbled on top.

If you can't get watercress...use rocket instead.

250g spaghetti
100g pitted dried black olives, chopped
8 canned anchovies, drained and cut into
    small pieces
Leaves picked from 1 small bunch of fresh
    flat-leaf parsley, chopped
Sea salt and freshly milled black pepper

FOR THE GARLIC CONFIT
250ml light olive oil
2 heads of garlic, broken into cloves and peeled

SERVES TWO

SPAGHETTI WITH GARLIC CONFIT AND OLIVES

First make the garlic confit. Pour the oil into a small pan and place over a very low heat. Add the garlic cloves. Leave to cook very gently for 2 hours. At the end of this time, the garlic will have turned slightly golden and will be very soft but still holding its shape.

Drain the garlic, retaining the oil. Place the garlic in a blender with 50ml of the oil and pulse for 15 seconds to a coarse purée.

Coil the spaghetti into a large pan of boiling salted water. Boil for 10–12 minutes, or according to packet instructions, until *al dente*. Drain and return to the pan. Add the puréed garlic confit, olives, and anchovies, and toss over a medium heat with enough of the remaining garlic oil to combine all the ingredients together. Season well and toss in the parsley. Serve immediately.

RISOTTO RICE

A good risotto is judged on its consistency as much as its flavour, which is why it's so important to use the right rice. Italian carnaroli is one of the best, and you can get it easily at Italian delicatessens and most good supermarkets. When cooked, carnaroli has a creamy texture with a nutty bite, and it makes a risotto as it should be – moist but not sloppy, and never stodgy.

100g unsalted butter, diced
400g risotto rice
100ml dry white wine
About 1 litre chicken or vegetable stock,
    heated until gently simmering
200g leeks (white part only), thinly sliced
    on the diagonal
A few bay leaves and fresh thyme sprigs
100g Parmesan cheese, freshly grated
200g new potatoes, boiled in their skins
    and lightly crushed
A handful each of fresh chervil and mint
    leaves, chopped

SERVES FOUR Sea salt and freshly milled black pepper

LEEK AND POTATO RISOTTO

Melt half of the butter in a large, deep, wide pan over a medium heat. Add the rice and stir for 2 minutes. Splash in the wine and mix well, then pour in a ladleful of the hot stock. Turn the heat down to medium-low. Cook for 15–20 minutes, stirring regularly and adding the stock ladle by ladle as the rice soaks up each addition. Add the leeks, bay leaves, and thyme sprigs after 5 minutes of cooking.

When the rice is almost *al dente*, stir in the Parmesan and remaining butter, and add a little extra stock. Remove and discard the bay leaves and thyme sprigs, then stir in the potatoes, chervil, and mint. Remove from the heat, check for seasoning, and serve immediately.

100g unsalted butter, diced
400g risotto rice
1tsp smoked paprika
100ml dry white wine
About 1 litre chicken or vegetable stock,
    heated until gently simmering
1 red pepper, sliced
1 yellow pepper, sliced
2tbsp olive oil
200g piece of chorizo sausage, skinned
    and diced
50–75g Parmesan cheese, freshly grated
1 small bunch of fresh chives, chopped
Sea salt and freshly milled black pepper

SERVES FOUR

SPICY CHORIZO AND PEPPER RISOTTO

Melt half of the butter in a large, deep, wide pan over a medium heat. Add the rice and paprika and stir for 2 minutes. Splash in the wine and mix well, then pour in a ladleful of the hot stock. Turn the heat down to medium-low. Cook for 15–20 minutes, stirring regularly and adding the stock ladle by ladle as the rice soaks up each addition.

While the risotto is cooking, fry the peppers in the oil in a separate pan for about 5 minutes until softened. Stir in the chorizo, then remove from the heat.

When the risotto is almost *al dente*, add the remaining butter and the Parmesan, then stir through the peppers and chorizo. Allow to heat gently. Remove from the heat, stir in the chives, and check for seasoning, then serve immediately.

1 head of garlic
About 30 cherry tomatoes
Olive oil
About 20 mini mozzarella balls, about 150g total weight
A handful of young, fresh marjoram sprigs
825ml chicken or vegetable stock
175ml tomato juice (from a can or carton)
100g unsalted butter, diced
400g risotto rice
100ml dry white wine
2tbsp tomato purée
75g Parmesan cheese, freshly grated
Sea salt and freshly milled black pepper

SERVES FOUR

TOMATO AND MOZZARELLA RISOTTO

Heat the oven to 200°C fan (220°C/gas 7). Wrap the head of garlic in foil and roast for about 20 minutes until starting to soften. Put the tomatoes in a small roasting pan, toss in a little olive oil and sea salt, and place in the oven with the garlic. Continue to roast for 15 minutes.

Meanwhile, toss the mozzarella in a bowl with the marjoram and some black pepper; set aside. Mix the stock with the tomato juice and heat gently until simmering.

Melt half of the butter in a large, deep, wide pan over a medium heat. Add the rice and stir for 2 minutes. Splash in the wine and mix well, then pour in a ladleful of the hot stock mixture. Turn the heat down to medium-low. Cook for 15–20 minutes, stirring regularly and adding the stock ladle by ladle as the rice soaks up each addition. Stir in the tomato purée about halfway through the cooking.

When the rice is almost *al dente*, stir in the remaining butter and the Parmesan. Remove from the heat and gently stir in the mozzarella and roasted tomatoes, reserving some of the marjoram for later. If there are any tomato juices left in the roasting pan, splash in a little olive oil and scrape them up, then stir into the risotto. Keep hot.

Unwrap the garlic and separate into cloves. Add a whole clove or two to the risotto, then squeeze the flesh out of the remaining cloves and stir it in. Check for seasoning and serve immediately, with the reserved marjoram sprinkled on top.

TEA

Don't just think of tea as a drink – it's an invaluable ingredient in cooking as well. There's a huge variety of teas, and I've experimented with many different blends to find the best teas to cook with. Three of my favourites are Earl Grey and jasmine, both of which give a wonderful perfume and flavour, and chamomile, a tea that I've found to be perfect for smoking fish and meat.

**MAKES
EIGHT FILLETS**

40g chamomile tea leaves
80g Demerara sugar
80g rice (any type)
A little olive oil
4 mackerel, filleted and pin-boned (skin left on)

CHAMOMILE TEA-SMOKED MACKEREL

Mix the tea, sugar, and rice together. Divide into two equal piles, spaced well apart, in a deep, heavy roasting pan (use an old one that you can keep for smoking in the future). Set a metal rack over the top of the pan and brush the rack with olive oil. Brush the skin of the mackerel fillets with olive oil, too, then place the mackerel skin-side down on the rack. Oil and season the mackerel flesh. Tent the entire rack with foil, tucking it in securely all around the edges of the pan.

Place the pan over a medium to high heat, using two burners to get an even distribution of heat. Leave undisturbed for 3–4 minutes. As soon as a moderate amount of smoke begins to escape from under the foil, immediately remove the pan from the heat. Leave to stand for a minimum of 20 minutes before uncovering the pan. If not eating straightaway, the mackerel can be kept for up to 2 days in the fridge.

For the tastiest result...there needs to be a good amount of smoke, so if possible leave the pan to stand outside.

Duck breasts...can be smoked in the same way.

30g Earl Grey tea leaves
300ml milk
300ml whipping or double cream
7 large organic egg yolks
150g caster sugar

3 large organic egg whites

EARL GREY TEA ICE CREAM

Put the tea in a pan with the milk and 100ml of the cream and bring to the boil. Simmer for 1 minute, then strain into a clean pan and set over a medium heat. Whisk the egg yolks and 75g of the sugar in a bowl until smooth. Whisk in a little of the hot cream. Pour this mixture into the pan of tea cream and mix thoroughly with a wooden spatula. Stir over a low heat until the custard is thick enough to coat the spatula.

Strain the custard through a fine sieve into a shallow container. Cover the surface of the custard with cling film to prevent a skin from forming, and chill in the fridge until cold.

Whip the remaining 200ml cream to soft peaks. Whisk the egg whites to soft peaks, then slowly whisk in the remaining 75g sugar to make a meringue. Fold the tea custard and whipped cream together, then mix in one-quarter of the meringue. Fold in the remaining meringue until evenly combined.

Transfer the mixture to a freezer container, then cover with cling film and the lid. Freeze until firm – this should take 2–4 hours. There's no need to churn in an ice cream maker as the whipped cream and egg whites make this ice cream beautifully smooth. The ice cream can be kept in the freezer for up to 3 days.

30g jasmine tea leaves
150g caster sugar
1 bay leaf
250g dried apricots

SERVES FOUR

JASMINE
TEA-INFUSED
APRICOTS

Place the tea in a pan with the sugar, bay leaf, and 100ml water. Bring to the boil and boil for 2 minutes, then strain into a clean pan. Add the apricots and simmer very gently for 10 minutes.

Cool to room temperature before serving, or chill in the fridge. Serve as a snack with cheese, or as a dessert with cream, ice cream, natural yogurt, or crème fraîche.

As an alternative...use prunes or dried figs instead of apricots.

COFFEE

Useful in sweet recipes because you only need a small quantity to get a powerful punch, coffee adds instant richness without being creamy or heavy. For the best aroma and flavour, buy it freshly ground and use it quickly – or keep it in an airtight container in the fridge once you've opened the packet. Supermarkets have a huge choice, but for something a little different, buy from your local coffee shop.

3½tsp freshly ground coffee
100g walnut pieces or halves
100g plain white flour
50g soft unsalted butter
50g caster sugar
1 medium organic egg, beaten

MAKES TWENTY 100g milk chocolate, broken into pieces

COFFEE AND WALNUT COOKIES

Blitz the coffee, walnuts, and flour in a food processor until the mixture resembles very coarse breadcrumbs. Cream the butter with the sugar. Gradually mix in the egg, then fold in the flour mix until well combined. Roll the dough in cling film to form a log shape about 6cm in diameter. Chill for at least 1 hour until firm (preferably for 2–3 hours, or overnight).

Heat the oven to 170°C fan (190°C/gas 5). Grease a large baking tray, or two smaller trays.

Slice the log of dough into twenty 5mm-thick slices and lay them on the tray. Bake for 15 minutes. Leave to cool on the tray.

Transfer the cookies to a rack covered with greaseproof paper. Melt the chocolate and drizzle over the cookies with a fork. Leave the chocolate to set before serving.

You can use other nuts... Brazils, pecans, and blanched almonds are three of the best in these cookies.

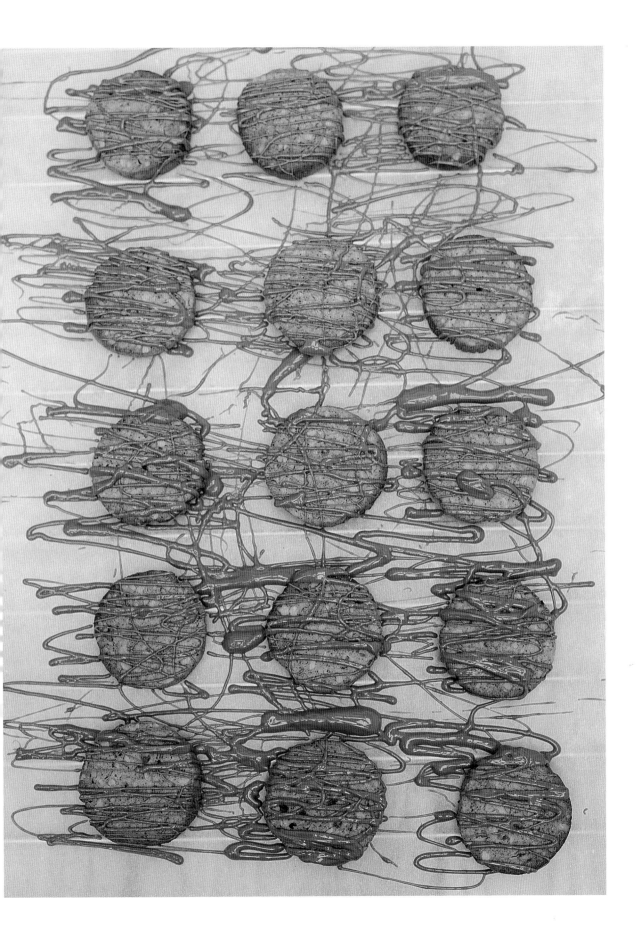

5 medium organic egg yolks
175g caster sugar
4 medium organic egg whites
250g mascarpone, beaten until smooth
200ml strong, cold espresso coffee
50ml Kahlùa (coffee liqueur)
Half a 200g packet of large sponge fingers
    (Italian *savoiardi* are best)
Cocoa powder, for dredging

SERVES SIX

TIRAMISU

Whisk the egg yolks with an electric mixer on medium speed until paler in colour and fluffy. Meanwhile, place 75g of the sugar and 40ml water in a small pan and bring slowly to the boil to dissolve the sugar. Boil rapidly for 3 minutes. Pour the sugar syrup slowly on to the egg yolks with the machine running. Continue whisking until the bowl no longer feels warm to the touch and the sabayon is pale and thick.

In another bowl, whisk the egg whites to soft peaks on high speed. With the machine running, slowly add the remaining 100g sugar and keep whisking to a stiff meringue.

Whisk one-third of the sabayon into the mascarpone until smooth, then gently fold in the remainder with a rubber spatula until evenly combined. Spoon half of the mascarpone sabayon over the meringue and mix well. Add the remainder and combine until smooth.

Mix the coffee and Kahlùa together in a wide bowl. Cut each sponge finger in half crossways, then in half again lengthways to get four pieces from each biscuit.

To assemble, put a small spoonful of the mascarpone mix in each of six Martini glasses (200–225ml capacity). Dip a piece of sponge finger into the coffee syrup, coating evenly and letting any excess drip off, then place in one of the glasses, with the cut side against the inside of the glass and the curved end at the top. Repeat until there are seven pieces of sponge in the glass, then spoon in more mascarpone mixture to fill the centre and all the gaps between the sponges. Smooth the top with a palette knife. Repeat with the remaining five glasses.

Cover each glass with cling film and refrigerate until ready to serve, preferably for 24 hours. Dredge with cocoa powder before serving.

FOR THE SPONGE
100g soft unsalted butter
100g caster sugar
2 medium organic eggs, beaten
1tsp instant coffee mixed with
    1tsp hot water
100g plain white flour, sifted
    with 1tsp baking powder

FOR THE BUTTERCREAM
1 medium organic egg beaten with
    2 medium organic egg yolks
75g caster sugar
125g soft unsalted butter, diced
1tsp instant coffee mixed with
    1tsp hot water

FOR THE GANACHE
100ml whipping or double cream
100g dark chocolate (70% cocoa
    solids), chopped
20g soft unsalted butter, diced

FOR THE GLAZE
2tbsp whipping or double cream
25g dark chocolate (70% cocoa
    solids), chopped
10g caster sugar
1tsp cocoa powder

SERVES SIX

GÂTEAU OPÉRA

Make the sponge. Heat the oven to 160°C fan (180°C/gas 4). Base-line and butter a large baking tray. Cream the butter and sugar, then whisk in the eggs and coffee, and fold in the flour. Spread into a 22 x 36cm rectangle in the baking tray, and bake for 4–5 minutes. Cool in the tray.

For the buttercream, whisk the eggs until thick and foamy. Dissolve the sugar in 2tbsp water, then boil for 3 minutes. Let the bubbles subside, then slowly pour the syrup down the side of the bowl on to the eggs with the machine running. Whisk until barely lukewarm, then whisk in the butter a piece at a time followed by the coffee. Cover with cling film.

Make the ganache. Scald the cream, pour it over the chocolate, and leave for 5 minutes. Beat until smooth, then beat in the butter a piece at a time. Cover the surface with cling film.

For the glaze, scald half of the cream and pour it over the chocolate. Dissolve the sugar with the cocoa, remaining cream, and 50ml water. Simmer for 2 minutes, then strain on to the chocolate and mix until smooth. Cover the surface with cling film; leave to cool and thicken.

Turn the sponge out of the tray and peel off the paper. Spread evenly with the buttercream, and chill for 30 minutes. Carefully spread the ganache over the buttercream; chill for 30 minutes.

With a hot knife, cut the rectangle in half, then trim into two squares. Cut each square into three rectangles. Chill for 10 minutes. Stack the rectangles on top of each other on a sheet of non-stick parchment. Trim the stack to give a neat finish. Chill for 10 minutes, then pour the glaze over the top and spread gently and evenly. Chill for 30 minutes.

Trim the sides of the cake with a hot knife and cut in half. Chill until serving time, then cut each cake into three pieces using a hot knife.

INGREDIENTS FINDER

The key ingredients in the book have their own sections, but many more ingredients feature prominently in the recipes. Use this handy finder to locate them – the bold type indicates the key ingredient they come under, and the italics refer to an alternative suggestion given at the end of a recipe. Page numbers are noted for easy reference.

ALMONDS: **Broccoli** and toasted almond pesto 15; Three-water **salmon** 72; Macaroons (**eggs**) 128; Spiced **apple** crumble cake 134; Rosemary roasted **pears** 158; Gooey chocolate slice (**dark chocolate**) 178; *Coffee and walnut cookies 214*

ANCHOVIES: Spaghetti with garlic confit and olives (**pasta**) 203

APPLES: Spiced red **cabbage** with apple 19

APRICOTS: *Peaches with rum and mint (**stone fruit**) 168; Chocolate and pistachio biscotti (**dark chocolate**) 176;* Jasmine **tea**-infused apricots 213

ASPARAGUS: Mousseline with asparagus (**eggs**) 126

AVOCADO: Shrimp and crab tian with avocado (**brown shrimps**) 82

BACON: **Broccoli** salad with bacon and pine nuts 16; **Pea** and bacon velouté 43; **Chicken** with bacon and pesto 108

BALSAMIC VINEGAR: balsamic toast in **Tuna** tartar with pickled cucumber 76; Baked goat's **cheese** with figs and walnuts 116; Balsamic **strawberries** with meringue 140

BEANS: **Pea** and broad bean salad with Manchego cheese 40; **Sole** with butter bean and chorizo hotpot 60; Seared **tuna** with white bean hummus 74; Lasagne with spinach and black beans (**beef**) 92

BEANSPROUTS: Asian coleslaw with chicken (**cabbage**) 20; **Prawn** laksa 66; Thai green **chicken** curry 109

BEETROOT: Goat's **cheese** and beetroot salad with praline 118

BLUEBERRIES: *Rhubarb fool with poached rhubarb 166*

BRAZIL NUTS: *Coffee and walnut cookies 214*

BROCCOLI: Thai green **chicken** curry 109

CABBAGE: Pan-fried haddock with creamy mustard cabbage (**white fish fillets**) 56

CAPERS: **Cauliflower** salad with caper and raisin dressing 28; in mayonnaise in **Sole** in beer batter 62

CARROTS: Asian coleslaw with chicken (**cabbage**) 20; Braised oxtail with red wine (**beef**) 90; Slow-roast shoulder of **lamb** with spring vegetables 97

CASHEWS: Linguine with rocket and cashew nut pesto (**pasta**) 200

CELERIAC: *Carrot and coriander galette 22; Cauliflower soup 31*

CHEESE: **Broccoli** soup with Stilton crumble 14; Three-**carrot** salad with feta 24; **Carrot** cake with cream cheese frosting 26; **Cauliflower** cheese with toasted cumin 30;

Mushroom and walnut dip 34; Red **onion** and blue cheese tart 38; **Pea** and broad bean salad with Manchego cheese 40; Crème fraîche cheesecake (**cream**) 122; Rosemary roasted **pears** 158; Penne with sunblush tomatoes and watercress (**pasta**) 202; Tomato and mozarella risotto (**risotto rice**) 206

CHICKEN: Asian coleslaw with chicken (**cabbage**) 20

CHICKPEAS: **Couscous** with spiced chickpeas and pineapple 181

CHOCOLATE: Macaroons (**eggs**) 128; Raspberries with white chocolate mousse (**berries**) 143; **Coffee** and walnut cookies 214; Gâteau Opéra (**coffee**) 218

CHORIZO: **Sole** with butter bean and chorizo hotpot 60; Spicy chorizo and pepper risotto (**risotto rice**) 205

COCONUT MILK: **Prawn** laksa 66; Thai green **chicken** curry 109

CONDENSED MILK: **Lemon** meringue slice 144

COURGETTES: Ratatouille (**aubergines**) 13

CRAB: **Shrimp** and crab tian with avocado 82

CREAM: Cherry **tomato** and mascarpone sauce 51; **Prawn** bisque 68; Baked **egg** custard 124; **Banana** caramel bavarois 136; **Banana** fritters with spiced cream 138; in toffee sauce in Baked **banana** puddings 139; Balsamic strawberries with meringue (**berries**) 140; Blackberry trifle (**berries**) 142; Raspberries with white chocolate mousse (**berries**) 143; **Mango** parfait 151; **Pineapple** tians with mascarpone and mint 162; **Rhubarb** and rosewater parfait 165; **Rhubarb** fool with poached rhubarb 166; Caramelized apricots with amaretti cream (**stone fruit**) 172; Chocolate ice cream (**dark chocolate**) 177; in sauce for Sticky toffee puddings (**golden syrup**) 189; Puy **lentils** with crushed potatoes and crème fraîche 194; Earl Grey **tea** ice cream 212; Tiramisu (**coffee**) 216

CUCUMBER: Asian coleslaw with chicken (**cabbage**) 20; **Tuna** tartar with pickled cucumber 76; Spicy **lamb** sticks with raita 96

CURRANTS: Eccles cakes (**dried fruit and nuts**) 198

DATES: Sticky toffee puddings (**golden syrup**) 189

DUCK: *Chamomile **tea**-smoked mackerel 208*

EGG: **Carrot** and coriander galette 22; Fried **mushrooms** and eggs on toast 32; Basil crème brûlée (**cream**) 121; **Banana** caramel bavarois 136; in custard in Blackberry trifle (**berries**) 142; **Lemon** meringue slice 144; **Mango** parfait 151; **Rhubarb** and rosewater parfait 165; Chocolate

INDEX

INDEX

223

ACKNOWLEDGMENTS

I must apologise to my loving wife Jane; I brought the entire book-making entourage into our home at such an important time in our lives. The fact that she managed to delay our daughter Jessie's birth until the last day of the shoot says it all. How thoughtful is that? Thank you, Jane.

Chantelle, thank you for your dedication. You worked day and night as sous chef in the restaurant, at the same time as helping me bring this book to life with your continuous research and development of new and creative ideas. It was a pleasure to have you in our home, and the boys have made a new special friend.

Thank you Mary-Clare, for encouraging me to write this second book, and supporting me all the way.

Congratulations to Alex, Emma, and Saskia at Smith & Gilmour for achieving the impossible – making this book look even more stunning than the first. Alex, your push for perfection has been amazing, jumping through hoops to get everything just right.

David, with seemingly little effort, you capture the image of the food or the moment perfectly every time. Why can't I see what you do when I look through the same lens? Thanks mate, you have become a good friend.

To my team at Pétrus, you know who you are, and you are worth more than two stars.

And now Jeni, my co-author. I hope I made it easier for you the second time around, and gave you what you wanted to put this book together. Thank you so much Jeni, you are a pleasure to work with and your attention to detail ensures that the writing on the page brings "the perfect ingredient" to life. Yet again you have done a wonderful job, continuing to be a huge support for me from start to finish. Love, Marcus.

DORLING KINDERSLEY WOULD LIKE TO THANK...

Angela Nilsen and the girls from Not Just Food for testing the recipes in the book so meticulously. Also thank you to Hilary Bird for the index.